The Ta

MW01134155

Image Reference & Species Accounts

Volume 1

Danny de Bruyne

A rarely seen mutation of the Sapphire Ornamental Tarantula - Poecilotheria metallica, displaying a double "folio" pattern on the abdomen.

Acknowledgments

My thanks go out to everyone that's worked with me, trusted me and been instrumental towards my
involvement, enjoyment and success not only in this hobby, but in publishing my first book.

Chriso Els and Dale Kindler for allowing me to photograph so many species in your collections.
André and Béanca Pretorius for the use of your lights, making many of these photos possible.
Lindie, because of you things like this can happen. Danny, because of you, they do.

Theraphosa stirmi - Burgundy Goliath Bird-Eater - Mature Female

Table of Contents

Acanthoscurria geniculata - Giant White Knee - Mature Male. This male is loading his pedipalps with sperm from a freshly made sperm web.

About the author

Among his other skills, Danny de Bruyne is a professional photographer and avid tarantula hobbyist with over 10 years of experience caring for and breeding tarantulas. He's the founder and owner of MyMonsters (PTY) Ltd., and also the designer and developer of http://www.mymonsters.co.za, a web based tarantula information resource and online shop designed and built in South Africa, which is also the foundation of this book.

Who this book is for

The Tarantula Gallery was created by a tarantula hobbyist for tarantula hobbyists and is by no means "the be all and end all" of tarantula publications, nor is it meant to serve as a scientific resource. This book is simply a collection of subjective opinions, information and images that have been compiled during more than 10 years of personal experience in the tarantula hobby by the author. This book is for anyone that will enjoy viewing high quality photographs of all the species herein or is simply interested to know a little more about the exotic world of keeping pet tarantulas.

Disclaimer

At the time of this writing (June 2020), all scientific and common names of the species mentioned in this book were current and correct to our knowledge and may change over time based on newer and more current discoveries or descriptions by taxonomists.

Every species and every specimen may behave differently or even exist differently in each hobbyist's experience, so the information in these pages should not be considered faultless. All husbandry info, including suggested enclosure temperatures, humidity and other basic enclosure requirements are to be considered as rudimentary and a good starting point. Each genus and species have very specific requirements and climates in their places of origin and it's the choice of each hobbyist to mimic those conditions perfectly in their enclosures or not.

Information regarding temperament, lifespan, type and behaviours of each species is purely derived from personal experience of the author and may differ from hobbyist to hobbyist or specimen to specimen. Tarantulas are wild creatures after all.

Enjoy.

Mature Female

SCIENTIFIC NAME	# Acanthoscurria geniculata
COMMON NAMES	Giant White Knee, Brazilian White Knee, White Banded Bird-Eater

ORIGIN Brazil

TYPE
New World, Terrestrial

TEMPERAMENT
Bold to defensive

LIFESPAN
Females (18 to 20 years) | Males (3 to 4 years)

ADULT SIZE
18cm to 20cm

GROWTH RATE
Fast

SUGGESTED ENCLOSURE TEMPERATURES
Winter (20 to 25°C) | Summer (25 to 28°C)

SUGGESTED ENCLOSURE HUMIDITY
60% to 80%

BASIC ENCLOSURE REQUIREMENTS: Terrestrial set-up with 5cm to 10cm of substrate, a large shelter and a water dish.

Acanthoscurria geniculata is well known in the tarantula hobby and a favourite choice when hobbyists are looking for a great display specimen. They're always out when your friends arrive and are voracious eaters, growing relatively fast between molts considering the sizes they reach. Seeing a full grown specimen up close is nothing short of impressive, quickly drawing the eye with it's striking black and white leg striping.

They grow to a formidable size around the 20cm (8in) mark. Acanthoscurria geniculata also get bolder as they get bigger. They don't scare easily and with many specimens you really have to annoy them before they flick urticating bristles or start getting defensive. You will find that they often stand their ground and face whatever is bothering them. If using large tweezers or other tool to nudge a full grown specimen along during maintenance, don't be surprised if it spins around and takes it from you, hoping for a meal.

This species really is quite strong at full size. You should make sure that their enclosures close properly and even latch because a full grown female is more than capable of lifting the lid of her enclosure if she can get her fangs under it.

Breeding is straight forward with this species and they don't require any special treatment to induce egg laying except raising humidity to a constant 80% or slightly more. Females can be very aggressive towards males during mating and due to their sheer strength, you will have a hard time protecting him if she chooses to attack. During mating, stay close with a tool you can use to protect the male, like your tweezers or 30cm ruler and be alert at all times.

Once the egg sac is produced, you may choose to pull it away from the female at around 6 weeks for manual incubation. An egg sac may contain anywhere upwards of 500 eggs, sometimes 800 and more.

Mature Female

SCIENTIFIC NAME	# Avicularia avicularia
COMMON NAMES	Common Pink Toe, South-American Pink Toe, Guyana Pink Toe

ORIGIN Guyana, Brazil

TYPE	TEMPERAMENT
New World, Arboreal, Webber	Docile and calm

LIFESPAN	ADULT SIZE	GROWTH RATE
Females (10 to 12 years)	Males (3 to 4 years)	12cm to 14cm	Medium to Fast

SUGGESTED ENCLOSURE TEMPERATURES	SUGGESTED ENCLOSURE HUMIDITY
Winter (20 to 24°C)	Summer (24 to 26°C)	70% to 80%

BASIC ENCLOSURE REQUIREMENTS: Arboreal set-up with good cross-flow ventilation, 5cm to 10cm of substrate and vertical structures like drift wood or curved cork bark in one corner as these arboreal tarantulas tend to create intricate webbed homes of their own. Use a larger water dish than usual and keep one corner of the enclosure moist to ensure good humidity.

One of the cutest species to own and a popular choice for everyone from beginners to experienced keepers (who usually have one or two hiding somewhere). The "Pink Toe" moniker suggests something cute and don't worry, the "common" pink toe, doesn't disappoint. Spiderlings/slings have pink legs with black tarsi/feet that look like little black boots, a metallic black carapace and an orange zig-zag pattern on their abdomen. As slings grow, these colours turn to metallic black, blue, green and purple tones. They're quite colourful when inspected closely under good lighting.

They're a gentle and docile species which, although we don't encourage, many hobbyists elect to handle. The chance of being hit with a poo missile or smeared with urticating hairs/ bristles from their abdomen will happen many times over before one of these beauties decide to deliver a bite or get defensive. If this species gets annoyed with a hobbyist trying to nudge it along during enclosure maintenance, it might aim it's abdomen in the direction of whatever is annoying it and squirt a poo in that direction, hilarious to witness. Also, if you get too close, instead of flicking urticating bristles like most new world tarantulas, they'll use their abdomen like a thumb and try rub them off on you instead. They're also jumpers, people handling them will find that they may jump to get away from the hot alien landscape that is our bodies, take precautions to ensure they don't fall to their death. With all the Avicularia species, humidity in the region of 60% to 80% must be maintained where possible along with good cross-flow ventilation to ensure a constant supply of fresh air, but not so much that it dries the enclosure out too quickly. Care should also be taken to ensure that it's not too wet and humid. A warm, humid and soupy environment will quickly stifle and kill your Avicularia.

Breeding is straight forward and mating usually goes ahead without much aggression from females towards mature males introduced to their enclosures. As long as the above suggestions for enclosure conditions are followed, there is a decent chance of your mated "avic" laying an egg sac. Expect anywhere from 80 to 200 eggs which can be incubated manually from about week 4.

Mature Female

SCIENTIFIC NAME	Avicularia juruensis
COMMON NAMES	Peruvian Pink Toe

ORIGIN   Nauta, Peru

TYPE	TEMPERAMENT
New World, Arboreal	Docile to nervous, can be bold

LIFESPAN	ADULT SIZE	GROWTH RATE
Females (10 to 12 years) | Males (3 to 4 years)	13cm to 15cm	Medium to Fast

SUGGESTED ENCLOSURE TEMPERATURES	SUGGESTED ENCLOSURE HUMIDITY
Winter (20 to 25°C) | Summer (24 to 26°C)	70% to 80%

BASIC ENCLOSURE REQUIREMENTS: Arboreal set-up with good cross-flow ventilation, 5cm to 10cm of substrate and vertical structures like drift wood or curved cork bark in one corner as these arboreal tarantulas tend to create intricate webbed homes of their own. Use a larger water dish than usual and keep one corner of the enclosure moist to ensure good humidity.

The Peruvian Pink Toe grows larger than your average pink toe and is much larger than Avicularia purpurea, the Purple Pink Toe for example. It has a beautiful light purple sheen on it's carapace and all over it's super-fuzzy body as well as dark purples on it's abdomen. Still docile for the most part, they can be a bit defensive and have been known to bite a careless keeper, but we have handled our full grown female unintentionally and she has never shown any aggression. When disturbing or trying to move this species, it won't flick urticating bristles at you, but will turn and start waving it's abdomen in your direction, trying to brush urticating bristles on to you instead. If you keep bothering it, you may fall victim to a squirt of poo as a message that you're really not welcome.

Avicularia juruensis requires an arboreal enclosure with humidity in the region of 70% to 80% with good cross-flow ventilation to ensure that air is always fresh. They web like crazy and will require structure in the upper areas of the enclosure to anchor their webbing. If you don't supply enough structure, they will probably web a suitable hammock-style den to hunt from anyway, but take care that they don't web up any ventilation holes that'll prevent them from getting fresh air.

They're really great eaters and have some pretty explosive feeding responses, in fact most keepers get bitten because they are cleaning the enclosure too gently and fool the spider in to thinking a careless finger is a potential meal. We absolutely adore all "pink toe" species and as far as we're concerned everybody should own them.

Breeding is not too complicated and females are generally tolerant of males. We've even left our male to co-habitate with our female for a few days to ensure regular matings take place. Don't leave him in there too long though or he may eventually become a meal. Egg sacs contain anywhere from 100 to 200 eggs and can be manually incubated from about week 4. If the female abandons her egg sac for any reason and does not return to it within a day, remove it immediately for manual incubation.

Mature Female

SCIENTIFIC NAME	Avicularia sp. Pucallpa
COMMON NAMES	Pucallpa Pink Toe

ORIGIN   River Ukajali, Pucallpa region, Peru

TYPE
New World, Arboreal, Webber

TEMPERAMENT
Docile to nervous

LIFESPAN
Females (10 to 12 years) | Males (3 to 4 years)

ADULT SIZE
12cm to 14cm

GROWTH RATE
Medium to Fast

SUGGESTED ENCLOSURE TEMPERATURES
Winter (20 to 25°C) | Summer (24 to 26°C)

SUGGESTED ENCLOSURE HUMIDITY
70% to 80%

BASIC ENCLOSURE REQUIREMENTS: Arboreal set-up with good cross-flow ventilation, 5cm to 10cm of substrate and vertical structures like drift wood or curved cork bark in one corner as these arboreal tarantulas tend to create intricate webbed homes of their own. Use a larger water dish than usual and keep one corner of the enclosure moist to ensure good humidity.

Avicularia sp. Pucallpa hasn't been officially described but currently falls under Avicularia juruensis morphotype #1 to our knowledge. This is a very colourful tarantula. On close inspection you'll find metallic green on the front legs, metallic purple on the abdomen, metallic yellow or gold on the carapace and of course a lovely light pink on the toes. A true beauty, inside and out. Calm and easy to work with but can be a bit jumpy if frightened.

They're webmasters in most cases, webbing thick silk lairs from which they stalk their prey. Good amounts of structure like drift wood from the substrate to a top corner of the enclosure should be made available for them to anchor their webbing. They don't enjoy large spacious enclosures with too little structure or with thin frilly plants or twigs. Remember, as with most Pink Toe species, good humidity with efficient cross flow ventilation are crucial to ensuring a suitable environment for these tarantulas. Many hobbyists misunderstand this requirement and keep this species in excessively high humidity, which does more harm than good. Always ensure that you have ventilation holes in your enclosure that cover different heights so that they promote the natural flow of air in and out of the enclosure.

Breeding this species is reasonably straight forward and no funny business or excessively aggressive behaviour is common from the females. Avicularia sp. Pucallpa also tends to have good fertility rates and produce egg sacs exceeding 200 slings at times. Eggs sacs can be removed from the female from about week 4 for manual incubation but can also be left with the females until slings reach second instar as they display good motherly instincts.

Mature Male

Mature Female

SCIENTIFIC NAME	Brachypelma albiceps
COMMON NAMES	Mexican Golden Red Rump, Golden Red Rump

ORIGIN Mexico

TYPE
New World, Terrestrial

TEMPERAMENT
Docile, may flick urticating bristles

LIFESPAN
Females (18 to 20 years) | Males (4 to 5 years)

ADULT SIZE
15cm to 16cm

GROWTH RATE
Medium

SUGGESTED ENCLOSURE TEMPERATURES
Winter (22 to 24°C) | Summer (26 to 28°C)

SUGGESTED ENCLOSURE HUMIDITY
60% to 70%

BASIC ENCLOSURE REQUIREMENTS: Terrestrial set-up with 5cm to 10cm of substrate, a shelter and a water dish.

The Mexican Golden Red Rump is a beautiful, unique looking Brachypelma species. This is a fantastic beginner tarantula that offers it all. They are docile, hardy tarantulas that eat well, grow well and reach a good size.

The most striking element on this tarantula is the egg-shell colour of the carapace in-between jet-black legs and a black abdomen covered in red hairs/setae. Striking as they may be, they are a docile and calm species that rarely exhibit any defensive behaviour beyond flicking urticating bristles when feeling threatened. You can also expect your Brachypelma albiceps to be visible most of the time because they are not a shy species and will happily spend the bulk of their time out in the open for you and your guests to enjoy.

Breeding is not always as easy as other Brachypelma species. Although females might be a little feisty during mating, mating is straight forward and males will generally make it out alive especially with a little protection from the breeder. However, females can be a bit stubborn when it comes to producing egg sacs. The female should be fed well after a mating and the enclosure can be wet quite heavily to one side, but allowed to dry out completely as the female gets larger and more gravid with eggs.

A dried out enclosure with warm temperatures and humidity in the region of 40% to 50% seems to assist in triggering the females to lay, but different breeders seem to have different theories with varying results. Due to the stubborn nature of this species when it comes to laying eggs, slings don't come around that often and are usually pricey so it's a good idea to get your hands on some of these when you can.

Mature Pair During Mating

Juvenile Female

Brachypelma auratum

Mexican Flame Knee

ORIGIN   Mexico

TYPE
New World, Terrestrial, Opportunistic Burrower

TEMPERAMENT
Nervous, flicks urticating bristles

LIFESPAN
Females (20 to 25 years) | Males (4 to 6 years)

ADULT SIZE
14cm to 15cm

GROWTH RATE
Slow to Medium

SUGGESTED ENCLOSURE TEMPERATURES
Winter (22 to 24°C) | Summer (26 to 28°C)

SUGGESTED ENCLOSURE HUMIDITY
60% to 70%

BASIC ENCLOSURE REQUIREMENTS: Terrestrial set-up with 5cm to 10cm of substrate, a shelter and a water dish.

Another beautiful member of the Brachypelma genus. The Mexican Flame Knee is mostly covered in black setae/hairs with white/cream highlights around the carapace and at all the leg joints. Their most striking characteristic is the little orange-red flames seen on each "knee".

They can be very skittish as youngsters but calm down a little as they grow. Unfortunately, their nervous nature makes them a bit of a pain when it comes to flicking urticating bristles and maybe not the best choice for a beginner hoping to handle their tarantula. Opening the enclosure to feed them is sometimes enough of a trigger for them to flick their bristles in defense, but they don't get much more defensive than that. Further disturbance will usually cause them to scurry in to their shelter or cower in a corner, flicking more bristles.

The Mexican Flame Knee grows to a lovely size but takes quite a while to get there. They molt at regular intervals but increase little in size between each molt. Their eating behaviour can be quite varied, eating very well after a molt and slowing down quite a lot as their next molt approaches, as though their pre-molt stage is more protracted than other Brachypelma species.

They're opportunistic burrowers and love to bulldoze their enclosures as they make themselves comfortable. As adults you can expect them to be comfortable out in the open and make fantastic display tarantulas.

Breeding this species is also a bit more tricky than other Brachypelma species. With their slow growth rate alone, it takes much longer to get a mature breeding pair than with faster growing species in the genus. Once you have a pair, mating is straight forward and good feeding should be all it takes to get your females to lay an egg sac, but they can also be stubborn. Make sure to provide extra substrate and a large shelter, this may help in making the female feel safe enough to lay her eggs.

Mature Female

SCIENTIFIC NAME	Brachypelma boehmei
COMMON NAMES	Mexican Fire Leg, Mexican Rust Leg

ORIGIN   Mexico

TYPE	TEMPERAMENT
New World, Terrestrial, Opportunistic Burrower	Nervous, flicks urticating bristles

LIFESPAN	ADULT SIZE	GROWTH RATE
Females (18 to 25 years) | Males (4 to 5 years)	14cm to 16cm	Medium

SUGGESTED ENCLOSURE TEMPERATURES	SUGGESTED ENCLOSURE HUMIDITY
Winter (22 to 24°C) | Summer (26 to 28°C)	70% to 80%

BASIC ENCLOSURE REQUIREMENTS: Terrestrial set-up with 5cm to 10cm of substrate, a shelter and a water dish.

The Mexican Fire Leg is without a doubt one of the most attractive looking tarantulas in the hobby today, especially in a well designed and decorated enclosure. They're named after their fluffy looking "fiery" rust/red coloured legs that are accentuated by their black velvety femurs. Match this to a pale rusty/red carapace and a black abdomen covered with red setae/hairs and you have a tarantula everyone will gawk at.

They're a hardy species and great for beginners but unfortunately, they're not as "cuddly" as they look. They're a skittish to nervous species that's very prone to flicking urticating bristles for almost no reason as juveniles and adults. Our specimens would flick bristles at us from the moment we opened the enclosure to do any maintenance or feeding, it's really quite annoying because the itches that follow can be exhausting.

When they're not being defensive, they hang out in the open most of the time waiting for something to eat and make great display spiders. Their feeding responses can be quite vigorous too, followed by some awesome happy dances, making feeding time fun and exciting. They're also opportunistic burrowers and may spend a fair amount of time bull-dozing their enclosures or hiding out in their shelters or burrows.

Make sure to provide this species with a little more substrate than normal for bulldozing and burrowing as well as a slightly higher humidity than most Brachypelma species.

Breeding this species is pretty easy. Mating is straight forward and females rarely show heavy aggression towards approaching males, but be cautious none the less. There are no special requirements to induce egg laying except allowing humidity to drop slightly once the female is large and heavily gravid with eggs. Expect an egg sac to contain anywhere from 400 to 600 eggs and be prepared to do some finger-numbing work getting them all separately housed and fed.

Juvenile Female

SCIENTIFIC NAME	Brachypelma hamorii
COMMON NAMES	Mexican Red Knee

ORIGIN Mexico

TYPE
New World, Terrestrial

TEMPERAMENT
Docile, may flick urticating bristles

LIFESPAN
Females (20 to 30+ years) | Males (3 to 5 years)

ADULT SIZE
15cm to 16cm

GROWTH RATE
Medium

SUGGESTED ENCLOSURE TEMPERATURES
Winter (22 to 24°C) | Summer (26 to 28°C)

SUGGESTED ENCLOSURE HUMIDITY
60% to 80%

BASIC ENCLOSURE REQUIREMENTS: Terrestrial set-up with 5cm to 10cm of substrate, a shelter and a water dish.

This species is famous for a reason. Not only is it hardy and docile, it has amazing colours, will probably live for over 20 years and is a species many consider handling. It's also a celebrity from all it's appearances in films and TV shows over the years, particularly in the film "Arachnophobia", portrayed as the parents of the spiders killing everyone in town, which couldn't be more false. Due to their calm and docile nature, these are one of the most handled tarantulas in the hobby. Although they are prone to flicking urticating bristles from time to time and depending on the specimen, we've never seen or heard of any aggressive behaviour displayed by this species throughout the hobby at all. We've seen people walking around at shopping malls and pet shows with their Mexican Red Knee perched on their shoulder, giving them to various people to hold and the tarantula seems completely happy to play along. In an enclosure, they make one of the best species to keep as a display specimen with their size, gorgeous colouring and willingness to stay out in the open.

Expect to keep this spider for a large part of your life, because female life expectancy has been said to reach up to 30 years and more. For a bug, that's pretty impressive. Unfortunately, with this being one of the most popular species in the hobby, they're still being over-harvested from their natural habitat, landing them on the CITES red list and may be causing changes to the availability of this species in future, so where possible always buy hobby-bred specimens.

Mature Male

Breeding is also very easy with this species and no special requirements are needed for a female to produce an egg sac. Expect a rather large amount of eggs to be produced in a sac, which may contain anywhere from 400 to 1000 eggs. The egg sac can be removed and manually incubated from about week 5.

Juvenile Female

SCIENTIFIC NAME	Caribena laeta
COMMON NAMES	Puerto Rican Pink Toe

ORIGIN Cuba / Puerto Rico / US Virgin Islands

TYPE New World, Arboreal, Heavy Webber	**TEMPERAMENT** Nervous and defensive
LIFESPAN Females (8 to 12 years)	Males (2 to 4 years)	**ADULT SIZE** 11cm to 12cm **GROWTH RATE** Medium to Fast
SUGGESTED ENCLOSURE TEMPERATURES Winter (22 to 24°C)	Summer (24 to 26°C)	**SUGGESTED ENCLOSURE HUMIDITY** 70% to 80%

BASIC ENCLOSURE REQUIREMENTS: Arboreal set-up with good cross-flow ventilation, 5cm to 10cm of substrate and vertical structures like drift wood or curved cork bark in one corner as these arboreal tarantulas tend to create intricate webbed homes of their own. Use a larger water dish than usual and keep one corner of the enclosure moist to ensure good humidity.

Caribena laeta is a unique "Pink Toe" with it's overall blonde and gold appearance. The Caribena genus aren't as docile as other pink toes and are quite aggressive compared to those in the Avicularia genus. Caribena laeta are also quite small at adult size, measuring only 12cm or so. The Puerto Rican pink toe is also pretty shy, it will build a thick silken lair behind it's chosen vertical structure, seldom venturing out during the day unless it's enclosure is kept slightly darker and really nice and warm. Consider giving them lots of structure to web on and also add a lot of wide leaf plants to create an overall shady space in your enclosure which will make them feel safer to move around.

These arboreal tarantulas are voracious when it comes to feeding and will attack prey with explosive enthusiasm. You can expect them to be on the prowl for food every night and can easily be over fed, so feed in moderation to enjoy your Puerto Rican Pink Toe for as long as possible.

Arboreal tarantulas from the Avicularia, Caribena or Ybyrapora genus all require higher humidity in the region of 70 to 80% with good cross-flow ventilation to ensure a safe and comfortable habitat . However, care should be taken to ensure that it's not too wet, humid and warm, which will eventually stifle and kill your tarantula.

Breeding Caribena laeta is relatively easy. A male can be placed anywhere on the female's open enclosure and they will quickly make each other's location known with rapid tapping and vibrations from both specimens. They will seek each other out and mating will be quite thorough. A male might keep the female busy for 10 minutes or more until satisfied that his job is done. Protect the males once mating comes to a close as females can sometimes turn the male in to a post mating meal. Egg sacs are not very large and contain anywhere from 60 to 120 eggs, which can be removed for manual incubation around week 4 or 5.

Mature Female

SCIENTIFIC NAME	Caribena versicolor
COMMON NAMES	Antilles Pink Toe, Martinique Pink Toe Martinique Red Tree Spider

ORIGIN Island of Martinique, Caribbean

TYPE
New World, Arboreal, Webber

TEMPERAMENT
Bold, can be feisty

LIFESPAN
Females (11 to 12 years) | Males (2 to 4 years)

ADULT SIZE
13cm to 15cm

GROWTH RATE
Medium

SUGGESTED ENCLOSURE TEMPERATURES
Winter (20 to 24°C) | Summer (26 to 28°C)

SUGGESTED ENCLOSURE HUMIDITY
70% to 80%

BASIC ENCLOSURE REQUIREMENTS: Arboreal set-up with good cross-flow ventilation, 5cm to 10cm of substrate and vertical structures like drift wood or curved cork bark in one corner as these arboreal tarantulas tend to create intricate webbed homes of their own. Use a larger water dish than usual and keep one corner of the enclosure moist to ensure good humidity.

Considered to be one of the most beautiful showpieces in hobby, The Martinique Pink Toe remains an absolute favourite of many keepers, especially fans of arboreal species.

Although a little more bold and cheeky than it's pink toed Avicularia cousins, this tarantula remains a total pleasure to own. It starts life as an adorable fluffy blue spiderling, slowly changing to a flurry of reddish-purple hues and developing a metallic turquoise carapace as adult colouration settles in. They're heavy webbers and build silken hammocks as high as they can, from which they stalk their prey. Take care when working in their enclosures as slings and juveniles, we aren't the first to have experienced one of these little delights jumping on to you while you work, don't panic, they usually jump right off again as they don't seem to like human trees. Once they get larger, a little more care should be taken when doing any maintenance as adult females can be quite bold, attacking anything that could potentially be a meal. You can expect fantastic feeding responses from sling to adult.

When breeding Caribena versicolor, a mature male that's recently produced a sperm web can be placed at the entrance of a mature female's enclosure. If she's receptive, they'll exchange rapid vibrations and tapping, finding each other quite quickly. Males will take their time to ensure sufficient insertions are made but should be guarded as mating comes to a close as females are known to attack when mating is complete. If the female doesn't respond to a male's tapping, rather wait and try again a few days later. Smart males will leave the enclosure of an unwilling female. Stubborn males go to tarantula heaven.

Egg sacs contain anywhere from 80 to over 200 eggs and can be left with mom full term or can be manually incubated from about week 4.

Freshly molted spiderling

Mature Female

SCIENTIFIC NAME	Chilobrachys dyscolus
COMMON NAMES	Asian Smokey Earth Tiger, Burma Chocolate Brown

ORIGIN   Burma / Malaysia / Myanmar

TYPE	TEMPERAMENT
Old World, Fossorial, Webber	Nervous, defensive and very fast

LIFESPAN	ADULT SIZE	GROWTH RATE
Females (11 to 12 years) | Males (2 to 4 years)	13cm to 14cm	Fast

SUGGESTED ENCLOSURE TEMPERATURES	SUGGESTED ENCLOSURE HUMIDITY
Winter (20 to 24°C) | Summer (26 to 28°C)	60% to 80%

BASIC ENCLOSURE REQUIREMENTS: Fossorial set-up with 15cm to 20cm or more of substrate to allow for burrowing with lots of structure and a water dish.

The Asian Smokey is a fast growing, super-fast moving old world tarantula species. Being fossorial, it's unfortunately a pet hole and it will seldom venture outside of it's burrow except late at night or when on the prowl for a meal. This species is generally dark chocolate brown and also exists in an ".sp Vietnam Blue" variation with a velvety black or dark-tan appearance that has sheens of blue hidden beneath.

This is not a species to be trifled with and definitely not a good choice for inexperienced hobbyists. Chilobrachys dyscolus does not tolerate disturbances and will display a threat pose to make this clear with very little persuasion. They can also give no warning at all and decide to bolt out from their burrows if feeling threatened. If you happen to be in the way, there is a very good chance of a painful bite. Their venom is significantly painful, causing intense burning and nervous reactions under the skin.

Males display sexual di-morphism and look completely different to the females after their ultimate molt. Mating can be a very intense affair. A male placed in a female's enclosure will signal his presence by tapping and vibrating to entice the female from her burrow. A willing female will approach with intensity and the male will keep his front legs and pedipalps quite high to protect himself and with good reason.

Their embrace is quick and quite turbulent. As soon as the male is able to make an insertion the female will react violently and both specimens will turn in to a blurry entanglement of flailing legs. We suggest that you leave the male to his chances and don't try protect him for fear that the females fangs might find you instead. If you do try to protect him, make sure to use a very long thin tool that the female will have trouble climbing.

Expect a female to lay an egg sac containing anywhere from 150 to 250 eggs. The eggs can be left with the female until they hatch or can be pulled away and manually incubated from around 4 week after laying.

Mature Female

SCIENTIFIC NAME	Chilobrachys huahini
COMMON NAMES	Asian Fawn, Thai Red, Huahini Bird Spider, Huahini Bird-Eater

ORIGIN   Thailand / Malaysia

TYPE	TEMPERAMENT	
Old World, Fossorial, Webber	Nervous, defensive and very fast	

LIFESPAN	ADULT SIZE	GROWTH RATE
Females (11 to 12 years) | Males (2 to 4 years)	14cm to 15cm	Fast

SUGGESTED ENCLOSURE TEMPERATURES	SUGGESTED ENCLOSURE HUMIDITY
Winter (20 to 24°C) | Summer (26 to 28°C)	60% to 70%

BASIC ENCLOSURE REQUIREMENTS: Fossorial set-up with 15cm to 20cm or more of substrate to allow for burrowing with lots of structure and a water dish.

The Asian Fawn is another fast growing, super-fast moving old world tarantula species, sometimes dubbed the Asian "OBT" (Orange Baboon Tarantula, Pterinochilus murinus), which is also a very defensive old world baboon spider. Like many Chilobrachys species, Chilobrachys huahini does not tolerate disturbances and will display a threat pose to make this clear with little very persuasion. The Asian fawn is sometimes referred to as being "crazy" with high speed defensive and aggressive behaviours. Their bite and venom is significantly painful, reported to cause intense burning and nervous reactions under the skin.

Being fossorial, it will seldom venture outside of it's burrow or shelter except late at night or when on the prowl for a meal. If you do not provide them with deep substrate, the Asian Fawn will web heavily to create a safe shelter and you can provide them with lots of structure to make this possible.

Males display sexual di-morphism mainly in that they are smaller and more scrawny then females but look quite similar. Mating can be a very intense affair. A male placed in a female's enclosure will signal his presence by tapping and vibrating to entice the female from her shelter. A willing female will approach with intensity and the male will keep his front legs and pedipalps quite high to protect himself.

Asian fawn females seem to be slightly more tolerant of males when mating occurs but it's a 50/50. As soon as the male is able to make an insertion the female may or may not react violently. If she does, both specimens will turn in to a blurry entanglement of legs. We suggest that you leave the male to his chances and don't try protect him for fear that the females fangs might find you instead. If you do try to protect him, make sure to use a very long thin tool that the female will have trouble climbing.

Expect a female to lay an egg sac containing anywhere from 150 to 250 eggs. The eggs can be left with the female until they hatch or can be pulled away and manually incubated from around 4 weeks after laying.

Mature Female

SCIENTIFIC NAME	# Chromatopelma cyaneopubescens
COMMON NAMES	Green Bottle Blue Tarantula, GBB

ORIGIN Brazil / Paraguay

TYPE	TEMPERAMENT
New World, Terrestrial, Webber	Nervous, may flick urticating bristles

LIFESPAN	ADULT SIZE	GROWTH RATE
Females (12 to 14 years)	Males (3 to 4 years)	13cm to 15cm	Medium to Fast

SUGGESTED ENCLOSURE TEMPERATURES	SUGGESTED ENCLOSURE HUMIDITY
Winter (22 to 25°C)	Summer (25 to 28°C)	40% to 50%

BASIC ENCLOSURE REQUIREMENTS: Terrestrial set-up with 5cm to 10cm of substrate, a water dish and added branches or other structures which will be used for attaching webbing. This species prefers slightly lower humidity than usual.

A poster-child of the tarantula hobby, the Green Bottle Blue Tarantula is rewarding to own and absolutely beautiful. As spiderlings they have a golden carapace, tiger-patterned abdomen and pink legs with black feet/tarsi looking like little black shoes. These colours change as they grow and the final product is a true beauty, regularly extracting a "wow" or "that's amazing" from people that have never seen them before. They aren't a shy species either, making for a great display tarantula.

Spiderling

They don't usually display any defensive behaviour besides a raised abdomen or the occasional flick of urticating bristles, but handling isn't recommended. They're explosive and voracious feeders from sling to adult, growing at a fairly quick pace too. The "GBB" is also a webbing specialist, creating amazing webbed hammocks and tunnels that it uses to detect prey, making it's enclosure a show-piece on it's own. Make sure to include pieces of driftwood and various branches or structures in their enclosures to anchor their webbing, you won't be disappointed. Keep in mind, the GBB originates in a desert-like region so is more comfortable with lower humidity. In our experience, simply over-filling their water dish to wet the substrate around it provides sufficient humidity.

Breeding this species is tricky. Females can be very aggressive towards males so always be ready to protect the male. Once the male is introduced to the female's enclosure, she should respond to his vibrations and tapping with equal interest. If she doesn't and the male isn't smart enough to leave, remove him yourself or he may well become a meal.

Females tend to swell, gravid with eggs quite quickly in the weeks following a successful mating and will begin creating an egg sac around 2 or 3 months later. Expect an egg sac to contain anywhere from 100 to 250 eggs. The egg sac can be removed and manually incubated from about 4 to 5 weeks if you choose to pull it away from the female.

Mature Female

Cyriocosmus perezmilesi

Bolivian Dwarf Beauty

ORIGIN   Bolivia

TYPE	TEMPERAMENT
New World, Semi-Fossorial, Webber, Dwarf Species	Docile, sometimes skittish

LIFESPAN	ADULT SIZE	GROWTH RATE
Females (5 to 7 years)	Males (1 to 2 years)	4cm to 5cm	Fast

SUGGESTED ENCLOSURE TEMPERATURES	SUGGESTED ENCLOSURE HUMIDITY
Winter (22 to 24°C)	Summer (25 to 28°C)	60% to 80%

BASIC ENCLOSURE REQUIREMENTS: Terrestrial set-up with 5cm to 10cm of substrate, a water dish and added branches or other structures which will be used for attaching webbing.

Another cute tarantula species in the genus Cyriocosmus and just as cute as it's cousin, Cyriocosmus elegans. This little Bolivian beauty has an adorable tiger pattern with a shiny peach coloured, heart-shaped bristle patch on it's black velvety abdomen. Cyriocosmus perezmilesi is a docile species and although it can be slightly twitchy and very quick when it does decide to run for cover, it's generally bold enough to hang about when there is a disturbance in the enclosure.

As a fossorial species that likes to burrow, they also web a lot above ground and are still very active and often visible, making them a great specimen overall for beginners.

Their small size means their enclosure doesn't take up too much space and they're pretty easy to maintain. Make sure to allow a fair amount of substrate in the enclosure so they can create a burrow to their liking, but also provide some structure for them to attach all their webbing. If you can get your hands on one of these, they are most certainly a fantastic addition to your collection.

Breeding Cyriocosmus perezmilesi is reasonably easy and straight forward. Females remain docile and rarely show any aggression towards a mature male that's introduced to the enclosure, but be alert just in case. The female will usually seal herself away to lay her egg sac within a month or two following a successful mating. Eggs can be pulled away and manually incubated around 3 to 4 weeks later if you like. You can expect anywhere from 100 to 250 eggs depending on the particular specimen.

Mature Female

Cyriopagopus lividus / lividum

Cobalt Blue

ORIGIN   Myanmar, Thailand

TYPE	TEMPERAMENT
Old World, Fossorial, Webber	Defensive, bold and will bite

LIFESPAN	ADULT SIZE	GROWTH RATE
Females (10 to 12 years) | Males (2 to 4 years)	13cm to 14cm	Fast

SUGGESTED ENCLOSURE TEMPERATURES	SUGGESTED ENCLOSURE HUMIDITY
Winter (20 to 24°C) | Summer (24 to 28°C)	60% to 80%

BASIC ENCLOSURE REQUIREMENTS: Fossorial set-up with 20cm to 25cm or more of substrate to allow for burrowing with some added structure and a water dish.

One of the best known names in the hobby, the Cobalt Blue has always been at the top of the list for many keepers and breeders. This fossorial old world species loves spending it's time below ground, only surfacing at night or when food items are on offer. They eat very well and grow fast. We've had male specimens grow from sling to maturity in one year flat, without power-feeding. Females take a little longer but once above 3cm, growth between molts will surprise you.

The fact that you scarcely see them doesn't seem to put any of us off getting one, because when you catch a glimpse of it in all it's blue glory, the name Cobalt Blue truly does it's name justice. Their entire bodies appear as black velvet, but provide some good lighting and you'll be spoiled to a beautiful range of blue hues over it's body with a darker tiger pattern on the abdomen. It's carapace can vary from a grey-ish blue to a creamy-blue depending on the specimen. When they are out and about, they can be extremely and explosively defensive. Sitting dead still one moment and fluttering to defense mode the next. It doesn't take much to see a threat pose displayed by a Cobalt Blue tarantula, they're definitely not to be considered for keeping by inexperienced hobbyists, especially adult specimens. They are solid burrowers and will make use of deep substrate to construct thickly webbed tunnels from which to hunt and take shelter. They will often web above ground as well if you provide some leaf litter or sphagnum moss with some structure like thick sticks or twigs.

Although this is quite a defensive species, breeding is not too complicated and females are quite tolerant of males approaching them for mating, but always be ready to protect the male if you must. Egg sacs usually contain upward of 80 eggs and can also be manually incubated from around week 4.

Mature Female

SCIENTIFIC NAME	Davus pentaloris
COMMON NAMES	Guatemalan Tiger Rump, Wasp Tarantula

ORIGIN Guatemala / Panama / Mexico

TYPE	TEMPERAMENT
New World, Semi-Fossorial, Webber, Dwarf Species	Skittish, flicks urticating bristles

LIFESPAN	ADULT SIZE	GROWTH RATE
Females (10 to 11 years)	Males (3 to 4 years)	9cm to 10cm	Fast

SUGGESTED ENCLOSURE TEMPERATURES	SUGGESTED ENCLOSURE HUMIDITY
Winter (18 to 22°C)	Summer (24 to 26°C)	60% to 80%

BASIC ENCLOSURE REQUIREMENTS: Terrestrial set-up with 10cm to 15cm of substrate with some added structure, a shelter and a water dish.

You will often see this species described in text and videos as Cyclosternum fasciatum or it's newer scientific name, Davus fasciatus – The Costa Rican Tiger Rump. In our findings, this is incorrect. The Tiger Rump originating in Guatemala with a red/copper carapace, the species most of us have come to know in the hobby and is pictured here, is actually Davus pentaloris, the Guatemalan Tiger Rump.

The Tiger Rump originating in Costa Rica and Panama with a black carapace and inverted colors on the abdomen is Davus fasciatus, the Costa Rican Tiger Rump, which is rarely seen in the hobby.

Either way, both are gorgeous and although they are pesky flickers of urticating bristles, the Guatemalan Tiger Rump is a great choice for beginners looking to add some interesting colours to their collections. Black legs with contrasting hues of reds, pinks an oranges from the carapace and abdomen of this species make it a striking and beautiful tarantula. Blue iridescence can also be seen on a freshly molted adult female like the one pictured here. They are a dwarf species and don't grow very large as far as tarantulas go, small enough to keep on your desk at work.

They're opportunistic burrowers but often spend time out in the open or on the prowl for food, a beautiful sight when out on display. They usually have great feeding responses too, making them fun to watch at feeding time. Sadly, their skittish, nervous nature mean that they will bolt for cover if disturbed and as mentioned above, excessive action around them will result in urticating bristles being flicked as added defense.

Mature males are slightly smaller and quite scrawny compared to mature females. Mating goes ahead quite smoothly but as always protect your mature male for future breeding attempts in case you have a feisty female on your hands. Egg sacs are produced anywhere from 2 to 3 months after a successful mating and can contain anywhere from 80 to 180 eggs depending on the female. The egg sac can be removed for manual incubation from around week 4 after laying.

Mature Female

SCIENTIFIC NAME	Encyocratella olivacea
COMMON NAMES	Tanzanian Black and Olive Baboon Spider

ORIGIN   Arusha & Usambara Regions, Tanzania

TYPE	TEMPERAMENT
Old World, Semi-Arboreal, Webber	Defensive, bold and will bite

LIFESPAN	ADULT SIZE	GROWTH RATE
Females (10 to 12 years) | Males (2 to 4 years)	13cm to 14cm	Fast

SUGGESTED ENCLOSURE TEMPERATURES	SUGGESTED ENCLOSURE HUMIDITY
Winter (20 to 24°C) | Summer (24 to 28°C)	60% to 80%

BASIC ENCLOSURE REQUIREMENTS: Terrestrial set-up with 5cm to 10cm of substrate with vertical structures like hollow drift wood or curved cork bark and a water dish.

A beautiful, typical old world baboon spider that's striking in looks and attitude. Encyocratella olivacea has stunning contrast where it's black velvety femurs meet the bright yellow joints at the patella/knees. The rest of it's legs are a slightly duller yellow or olive colour with tiny black spots nearer the tarsi/feet. It's abdomen is also a lovely deep yellow with the typical dark spotted "skull" pattern seen on other baboon spiders like Heteroscodra maculata and Pterinochilus murinus. They are just as feisty too with a typical old world attitude.

Certain specimens will display a threat pose when you simply approach their enclosure and will happily stand and fight, attack and bite anything that gets too close. They can move quickly when they need to, so great care should be taken when working with this species because an envenomed bite would be significantly unpleasant. The venom of Encyocratella olivacea is suspected to have similar potency to Pterinochilus murinus, the Usambara Orange Baboon Tarantula, which is known to cause severe pain and cramping many days or even weeks and months after being bitten.

We find that the best enclosure for this species includes a fair amount of substrate with a hollow branch, hollow piece of cork bark or tube of bamboo plunged right to the base of the enclosure. The Black and Olive Baboon spider will probably excavate most of the substrate from inside this hollow hideout and then line it heavily with webbing from top to bottom, creating a home that is both beneath and above the substrate.

Mating this species can bring out their arboreal tendencies. Males tend to be nervous around a female and will attempt to lure her away from her shelter if possible. He will lead her around with constant tapping, attempting to get her above him on vertical surface. Once he's happy, he will engage her to attempt insertions. Females are generally calm during mating but stay close to protect him in case she attacks. Encyocratella olivacea is one of very few species who's females do not possess spermatheca, sperm is stored in the oviducts and uterus instead, meaning that if the female molts, sperm inserted by a male during mating will not be lost. Egg sacs are fixed to their shelters instead of carried loosely and will contain about 80 to 120 eggs in most cases. Females can be temperamental so manual incubation of the eggs is recommended as early as possible.

Mature Female

SCIENTIFIC NAME	# Ephebopus cyanognathus
COMMON NAMES	Blue Fang Tarantula, Blue Fang Skeleton

ORIGIN   French Guiana

TYPE	TEMPERAMENT
New World, Fossorial, Webber	Nervous and defensive

LIFESPAN	ADULT SIZE	GROWTH RATE
Females (12 to 15 years) | Males (3 to 4 years)	12cm to 13cm	Fast

SUGGESTED ENCLOSURE TEMPERATURES	SUGGESTED ENCLOSURE HUMIDITY
Winter (22 to 24°C) | Summer (24 to 28°C)	70% to 80%

BASIC ENCLOSURE REQUIREMENTS: Fossorial set-up with 15cm to 20cm (or more) of substrate to allow for burrowing with added structure for webbing and a water dish.

The Blue Fang is a colourful, beautiful and popular tarantula despite it's tendency to be a pet hole. Even as spiderlings they have bright blue fangs, a gray carapace and a metallic green abdomen. Their little legs are mostly pink, leading to yellow striped joints just before their black tarsi/feet, giving them the appearance of wearing black shoes. These colours fade as the spider grows but adults are still a beauty to behold, when they appear of course.

Blue fangs rarely bask out in the open. If provided with nothing more than deep substrate and a water dish, they'll make quick work of digging a deep tunnel network to call home. They make good use of leaf litter, twigs or sphagnum moss placed in the enclosure to create a spouted entrance to their burrow entrances. The enclosure for blue fangs should include some arboreal elements when young as they tend to prefer a vertical shelter with a small burrow leading in to the substrate, however this diminishes with age and they

eventually follow a strictly fossorial lifestyle. Their defensive nature makes them a handful to maintain at times, known to occasionally display a threat pose when approached. Unlike most new world tarantulas, it's urticating bristles are found on it's pedipalps and femurs. When annoyed enough it will flick urticating bristles and won't hesitate to bite.

Breeding Ephebopus cyanognathus is straight forward if environmental factors are maintained. Females can be ruthless so males should be protected. Males will attempt to lure a female out from her burrow with constant tapping, sometimes diving right in to go fetch her. This can be stressful because he can't be protected while down there. Once he has her out in the open mating takes place quite swiftly and a healthy egg sac should follow a few months after a successful mating attempt. You can expect an egg sac to contain anywhere from 80 to 160 eggs.

Mature Female

Ephebopus murinus

Skeleton Tarantula, Yellow Knee Skeleton

ORIGIN Brazil / Suriname

TYPE	TEMPERAMENT
New World, Fossorial, Webber	Nervous to bold and defensive

LIFESPAN	ADULT SIZE	GROWTH RATE
Females (12 to 15 years) | Males (3 to 4 years)	12cm to 13cm	Fast

SUGGESTED ENCLOSURE TEMPERATURES	SUGGESTED ENCLOSURE HUMIDITY
Winter (22 to 24°C) | Summer (24 to 28°C)	70% to 80%

BASIC ENCLOSURE REQUIREMENTS: Fossorial set-up with 15cm to 20cm (or more) of substrate to allow for burrowing with added structure for webbing and a water dish.

Also known as the platypus of tarantulas and similar to the Blue Fang Tarantula, the Skeleton tarantula has it all upside down. A new world species that's from the arboreal Avicularinae sub-family (like Pink Toes), yet lives a fossorial life deep underground. Also, most new world species have their defensive urticating bristles on their abdomen, but Ephebopus murinus has them on it's pedipalps. By rapidly rubbing it's pedipalps against it's fangs, it can flick the bristles in the direction of potential threats.

The skeleton is a gorgeous looking tarantula. As slings, they have green colouration with blonde hairs on their abdomens and already have skeleton patterns on their legs. As adults, their carapace turns to the color of bone, matching the skeleton patterns on it's legs. Sadly, being fossorial "pet holes" like the Blue Fang, they spend most of their time in their burrows, only showing their front legs at night or when hungry for prey. They are not to be trifled with, their nervous and defensive attitude will lead to a bite if the hobbyist is

careless. Consider adding some leaf litter or sphagnum moss to their enclosures, they will gather this at the mouth of their burrows which will eventually take on a short turret shape.

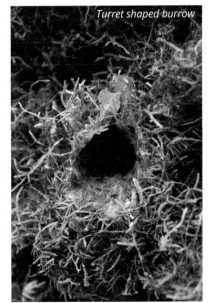
Turret shaped burrow

Breeding Ephebopus murinus is straight forward if environmental factors are maintained. Females can be ruthless so males should be protected. Males will attempt to lure a female out from her burrow with relentless tapping, sometimes diving right in to go fetch her. This can be stressful because he can't be protected while down there. Once he has her out in the open, mating takes place quite swiftly and a healthy egg sac should follow a few months after a successful mating attempt. You can expect an egg sac to contain anywhere from 80 to 150 eggs.

Mature Female

SCIENTIFIC NAME	Eupalaestrus campestratus
COMMON NAMES	Pink Zebra Beauty

ORIGIN   Brazil / Paraguay / Argentina

TYPE
New World, Terrestrial

TEMPERAMENT
Docile and calm

LIFESPAN
Females (16 to 20 years) | Males (5 to 6 years)

ADULT SIZE
12cm to 13cm

GROWTH RATE
Slow to Medium

SUGGESTED ENCLOSURE TEMPERATURES
Winter (18 to 24°C) | Summer (24 to 28°C)

SUGGESTED ENCLOSURE HUMIDITY
65% to 75%

BASIC ENCLOSURE REQUIREMENTS: Terrestrial set-up with 5cm to 10cm of substrate, a shelter and a water dish.

The Pink Zebra Beauty is quite a common name in the hobby but sometimes hard to get your hands on. This is a very docile and hardy tarantula which is also a very good choice for beginners. They are also quite pretty with their combination of a cream coloured carapace, "Zebra" striping on their legs and light pinkish setae/hairs covering most of the body.

The Pink Zebra Beauty is sometimes referred to as a pet rock because they seem to have endless patience and a very laid back attitude overall. They will sit out in the open for ages and do not get startled very easily.

When young, they might be a little skittish or nervous but this changes as they grow. They become much calmer as they get bigger but take note that they grow slowly, increasing little in size between molts, so you might want to buy them as juveniles or at a decent size already if possible. They don't grow extremely large, but make great display tarantulas and are very easy to maintain and work with.

This species can sometimes be a bulldozer and re-decorator. They will not only move things around, but they'll dig up whole areas of substrate, creating bunkers and mounds all over the place as they see fit, so if your specimen displays these characteristics, give them loads more substrate to play around with.

Eupalaestrus campestratus is also quite laid back when it comes to breeding and seems to breed better if the females are living in larger enclosures with deeper substrate. Males should be protected as always just to keep them safe in case of a sudden attack. Males will begin their sequence of tapping and vibrating once introduced to the female's enclosure.

Females generally approach calmly and willingly. If mating is successful, egg sacs contain up to 1000 small eggs, so be prepared for some hard work. Survival rates for eggs vary greatly and in bad cases there is a chance that only 20 to 30% survive to third instar.

Mature Female

SCIENTIFIC NAME	Grammostola porteri
COMMON NAMES	Chilean Rose NCF, Rose Tarantula NCF
	NCF: Normal Colour Form

ORIGIN   Northern Chile

TYPE
New World, Terrestrial

TEMPERAMENT
Docile to nervous

LIFESPAN
Females (20 to 25 years) | Males (4 to 5 years)

ADULT SIZE
14cm to 16cm

GROWTH RATE
Slow to Medium

SUGGESTED ENCLOSURE TEMPERATURES
Winter (20 to 22°C) | Summer (25 to 28°C)

SUGGESTED ENCLOSURE HUMIDITY
50% to 60%

BASIC ENCLOSURE REQUIREMENTS: Terrestrial set-up with 5cm to 10cm of substrate, a shelter and a water dish.

Another of the "teddy bears" in the tarantula hobby and also a common first tarantula for many keepers due to it's calm and docile nature. It's fluffy gray to pink appearance and iridescent rose coloured carapace make this a beautiful spider. These are very slow living tarantulas, moving around very little and usually out on display making them great display specimens.

Generally, the Chilean Rose tarantula eats voraciously, but is known to go on fasts or hunger strikes before and after a molt, but also at random times, don't panic. Fasting is completely normal for tarantulas and more so with the Chilean Rose which can fast for months on end, leaving their owners worried that they might die or suffer from malnutrition. But fear not, they will start eating when they're good and ready again. The only other reason a tarantula stops eating is if it's unwell or there are serious problems in the enclosure like bacteria or an infestation of pests, like mites. If your Chilean Rose suddenly stops taking food, just make sure your enclosure is clean, well maintained and has all the suitable conditions. Try feeding again once every two weeks and remove any uneaten feeders if they aren't eaten within a day or two.

Take Note: It is generally known that the Chilean rose is a very docile and calm tarantula, but as with any species, get to know your own specimen. We've witnessed a few specimens that simply go against the grain and have become very defensive, often throw a threat pose and even try to bite. Nobody knows why this happens with certain specimens, so pay attention to the nature of your specific tarantula and take great care if you decide to handle it.

Breeding Grammostola porteri is relatively easy and no special conditioning is needed for a female to be receptive other than being well fed. Mating goes ahead without too much drama but as always, protect the male as females can be slightly feisty. If mating is successful, egg sacs contain upward of 500 eggs so be prepared to house a lot of slings once they hatch. They are generally good parents so you can leave the egg sac with the mom full term until they emerge as slings or pull it away around 4 to 5 weeks after laying for manual incubation.

Mature Female

SCIENTIFIC NAME	# Grammostola pulchra
COMMON NAMES	Brazilian Black

ORIGIN   Brazil

TYPE	TEMPERAMENT
New World, Terrestrial	Docile and calm

LIFESPAN	ADULT SIZE	GROWTH RATE
Females (20 to 25+ years) | Males (4 to 5 years)	14cm to 16cm	Slow to Medium

SUGGESTED ENCLOSURE TEMPERATURES	SUGGESTED ENCLOSURE HUMIDITY
Winter (20 to 22°C) | Summer (25 to 28°C)	50% to 60%

BASIC ENCLOSURE REQUIREMENTS: Terrestrial set-up with 5cm to 10cm of substrate, a shelter and a water dish.

An absolute must for your collection and a black beauty among all tarantulas. The Brazilian Black is famous for being one of the most docile of all tarantulas, it has a very calm temperament in general, only skittish as youngsters but becoming gentle giants as they mature.

Grammostola pulchra also have a very long lifespan, living well over 20 years with some claiming they can live up to 40 years or more. Grammostola pulchra is not shy and makes a good display tarantula with it's uncommon and strikingly beautiful satin-black colouring, especially directly after a molt. Due to their stubborn breeding habits they can be hard to find at times and are usually pricey, but worth every penny. Both males and females can be rather good at bulldozing their enclosures. They even flip their water dishes upside down, pick them up and place them somewhere else, or just bury them, so keeping a topped-up water dish in their enclosure can be a constant challenge.

Even though mating goes ahead quite easily, the Brazilian Black can be difficult to breed successfully and is the reason for their occasional scarcity and higher price tag. A number of breeders have commented that this species needs to go through a cold winter, so the breeder may choose to either wait for winter and expose the tarantula to the colder temperatures or place it in an artificially cooled environment for a few "winter" months.

Once the winter period has passed, a gradual warming up ending with a humid "rainy" period seems to assist in triggering females to produce egg sacs, but it seems nobody has this down to an accurate art as yet. Breeders that have mated four or five females might get an egg sac from only one or maybe two of them if lucky.

Eggs from Grammostola pulchra are relatively large so there aren't as many eggs in a sac as one might expect from a Grammostola species. If mating was successful and the female indeed produces an egg sac, the breeder can expect anywhere around 80 to 150 eggs. The egg sac can be removed for manual incubation from around week 5 if desired. Due to the difficulty of breeding this species, it might be better to pull the sac away quite early for manual incubation to avoid any risk of the mother destroying or eating the egg sac.

Mature Female

SCIENTIFIC NAME	# Grammostola pulchripes
COMMON NAMES	Chaco Golden Knee

ORIGIN   Sub-Tropical Paraguay

TYPE
New World, Terrestrial

TEMPERAMENT
Docile and calm

LIFESPAN
Females (20 to 25+ years) | Males (3 to 4 years)

ADULT SIZE
15cm to 17cm

GROWTH RATE
Medium

SUGGESTED ENCLOSURE TEMPERATURES
Winter (20 to 22°C) | Summer (25 to 28°C)

SUGGESTED ENCLOSURE HUMIDITY
60% to 70%

BASIC ENCLOSURE REQUIREMENTS: Terrestrial set-up with 5cm to 10cm of substrate, a shelter and a water dish.

The best beginner species of all in our opinion and another of the tarantula "teddy bears", this is often the first tarantula for many keepers due to it's calm and docile nature. Most specimens are so docile that certain keepers elect to handle them from sling to adult. They rarely show nervous or skittish behaviour and also rarely flick urticating bristles. We don't promote the handling of tarantulas but whenever an adult Chaco Golden Knee crosses our path, it's not long before we're sitting on the couch letting it walk all over us.

Gold is definitely the theme for this tarantula, they have beautiful yellow to golden striped "knees" with fluffy light-pink setae/hairs over most of their dark brown bodies. The urticating bristle patch on the abdomen, sometimes referred to as their "mirror patch" also has a golden appearance. Their carapace is a lovely rich brown but has a golden metallic sheen to it that becomes more evident as the spider reaches adulthood. Really a stunner as a full grown specimen.

The Chaco Golden Knee also makes a great display tarantula because of it's bold and easy going nature, happy to sit out in the open most of the time. They generally eat really well and grow at a fair pace. They are also known to be re-decorators when younger, burying their water dishes, building burrows and mounds until they feel everything looks just right, they really are a pleasure to watch, keep and own.

Grammostola pulchripes is easy to breed and almost always available in the hobby. Males make their presence known with significant tapping of the pedipalps and also by bobbing up and down with their bodies. Mating generally goes quite smoothly but females can be quite boisterous towards males so they should be protected in case of a last moment snack attack from the female.

If mating is successful and the female produces an egg sac, it can be left with mom or removed around the 4 to 5 week mark for manual incubation. Expect a large amount of small eggs, numbering anywhere from 400 to 800 or more.

Mature Female

Hapalopus formosus

Colombian Pumpkin Patch, Pumpkin Patch Tarantula

ORIGIN Colombia

TYPE
New World, Terrestrial, Webber, Dwarf Species

TEMPERAMENT
Nervous, may flick urticating bristles

LIFESPAN
Females (8 to 10 years) | Males (3 to 4 years)

ADULT SIZE 7cm to 8cm

GROWTH RATE Medium to Fast

SUGGESTED ENCLOSURE TEMPERATURES
Winter (22 to 25°C) | Summer (25 to 28°C)

SUGGESTED ENCLOSURE HUMIDITY
60% to 70%

BASIC ENCLOSURE REQUIREMENTS: Terrestrial set-up with 5cm to 10cm of substrate, a water dish and added branches or other structures which will be used for attaching webbing.

An eye-catching dwarf tarantula species with a docile temperament, the Pumpkin Patch tarantula is one of those must-haves in any collection. The lovely pale orange and black "pumpkin" patterns on it's abdomen and the "keyhole" pattern on it's carapace give it the most adorable appearance.

This spider can even be recommended as a beginner species. Although they can be quite nervous, they are generally slow to get aggravated and rarely bite, but always get to know your own specimen. Their webbed lairs extend well beyond their main shelter where they often bask or lay in wait for a snack, making them a great tarantula to have on display.

They like to burrow as well so it's important to give them deep enough substrate to play around with. During pre-molt they may stay hidden in their shelter so don't worry if they disappear for a while, hopefully they will emerge in a month or so with a shiny new suit.

There are two varieties of this species, one grows to about 8cm and the other grows a little larger to about 12cm. Hobbyists sometimes name them Hapalopus sp. Colombia (Large) or Hapalopus sp. Colombia (Small), but are mostly identified by size once full-grown. Males of the small variety can be as small as 5cm and males from the large variety can reach 8cm or more. Unfortunately, many specimens we have in the hobby seem to be a hybrid of the two, neither small nor large, thus the assumption amongst hobbyists that they may have been extensively interbred. Breeders should be responsible and always try and match the correct males and females.

There are no special requirements for breeding this species except that females should be mated early in their molt cycle. Males will attract a female with constant tapping and vibrating but are nervous and will constantly back away from a keen female and with good reason. You should stay vigilant because females are known to try grab a post-mating snack. If mating was successful, the female will web herself shut in her shelter and produce an egg sac carrying around 80 to 150 eggs when ready. Spiderlings are tiny at 4mm to 5mm in size and will need very small feeders like flightless fruit flies or pinhead crickets.

Mature Female

SCIENTIFIC NAME	Harpactirella lightfooti
COMMON NAMES	Lightfoot's Lesser Baboon Spider

ORIGIN South Africa

TYPE
Old World, Fossorial, Webber, Dwarf Species

TEMPERAMENT
Nervous, can be defensive

LIFESPAN
Females (5 to 6 years) | Males (1 to 2 years)

ADULT SIZE
6cm to 7cm

GROWTH RATE
Fast

SUGGESTED ENCLOSURE TEMPERATURES
Winter (22 to 25°C) | Summer (25 to 28°C)

SUGGESTED ENCLOSURE HUMIDITY
50% to 60%

BASIC ENCLOSURE REQUIREMENTS: Fossorial set-up with 10cm to 15cm or more of substrate to allow for burrowing with some added structure and a water dish.

These little baboon spiders are sometimes seen running across the living room floor in the localities of the Cape provinces in South Africa where they are found. Of course, it's usually the males that are doing the running in search of females to mate with. Females are pretty static and once they find and build a webbed lair which is usually under rocks or cool sheltered structure, they seldom move about except to find food and usually in the dark. Being a Lesser-Baboon Spider, they are a dwarf species and adult females grow no larger than about 7cm. Males are smaller, reaching only around 5cm at maturity.

They are typical of the gorgeous golden baboon spiders of South Africa and have a slightly elongated and beautiful golden star-burst pattern on the carapace as well as the typical striped and spotted abdomen seen on many baboon species. Their darker abdomen markings start from the spinnerets as stripes, becoming spots nearer to the carapace.

They are heavy webbers, making great use of rocks, twigs and other structure to build their shelters from. If they can't find enough structure they will usually begin to burrow and create a tubular tunnel leading to a lair deeper down. They are skittish and quick moving baboon spiders, but are actually quite tolerant of disturbance. They will bolt when disturbed or touched but won't easily display a threat pose in defense unless really provoked and they will indeed bite if pushed too far. Their venom is said to be quite potent to mice and must be assumed to be like any other baboon spider venom, care should be taken not to get bitten as no conclusive tests have been done on humans. Expect the usual painful bite and possible muscle spasms or cramping caused by venom from baboon spiders.

There are no special breeding requirements as long as environmental conditions are maintained. Males often become a snack and should be protected during mating attempts. If mating is successful, the egg carrying female's abdomen will become plump and elongated.

She will produce an egg sac containing between 80 to 150 eggs which can be removed around 4 weeks later for manual incubation. However, they can be good moms and the egg sac can be left with the mother full term if you are willing to risk it.

Mature Female

SCIENTIFIC NAME: Heterothele villosella

COMMON NAMES: Tanzanian Chestnut, Tanzanian Chestnut Baboon Spider

ORIGIN Tanzania / East Africa

TYPE
Old World, Semi-Fossorial, Webber, Dwarf Species, Communal

TEMPERAMENT
Nervous to skittish

LIFESPAN
Females (5 to 6 years) | Males (1 to 2 years)

ADULT SIZE
5cm to 6cm

GROWTH RATE
Fast

SUGGESTED ENCLOSURE TEMPERATURES
Winter (22 to 25°C) | Summer (25 to 28°C)

SUGGESTED ENCLOSURE HUMIDITY
50% to 60%

BASIC ENCLOSURE REQUIREMENTS: Fossorial set-up with 10cm to 15cm or more of substrate to allow for burrowing with some added structure and a water dish.

If you were looking for an old world tarantula that could be called easy to work with, possibly even for a beginner, this is a good option.

The Tanzanian Chestnut is a beautiful dwarf species among baboon spiders. It has an interesting pattern on it's abdomen and a stunning black and pale-yellow pattern on the carapace, looking like a nut that was broken in half.

Considered to be a beginner species by certain hobbyists, Heterothele villosella is a skittish but even-tempered spider which is slow to anger or get defensive. As with all baboon species, being frightened or provoked may result in a threat display or even a bite. With Heterothele villosella the first thing to follow a threat pose is usually a sprint in the opposite direction. But don't get too brave, their fangs still work and they will not hesitate to use them if feeling threatened.

To make this species even more interesting, it's one of the few with true communal tendencies, capable of living together successfully. Just watch out for all the breeding that might take place without your assistance because your set-up could soon be over crowded. They are excellent spiders to look after and observe.

They breed relatively easily with no special requirements and will breed continuously in a communal set-up. Egg sacs contain anywhere from 50 to 100 eggs, resulting in dull little spiderlings with pale patches on their abdomens. Females make great mothers and will care for their egg sacs and spiderlings with the need for manual incubation.

Mature Female

Homeomma chilensis

Chilean Flame

ORIGIN   Between Maule and Biobio, Andes Mountains, Chile

TYPE	TEMPERAMENT	
New World, Semi-Fossorial, Dwarf Species	Docile but nervous	

LIFESPAN	ADULT SIZE	GROWTH RATE
Females (8 to 12 years)	Males (2 to 3 years)	7cm to 8cm	Slow

SUGGESTED ENCLOSURE TEMPERATURES	SUGGESTED ENCLOSURE HUMIDITY
Winter (22 to 24°C)	Summer (26 to 28°C)	60% to 70%

BASIC ENCLOSURE REQUIREMENTS: Terrestrial/Fossorial hybrid setup with a water dish, some driftwood or other structure, a slightly buried shelter as a starting burrow and roughly 10cm to 15cm of substrate to allow for deeper burrowing.

Previously known as Euathlus sp. red, sp. red flame and other red monikers, the Chilean Flame is now described as Homeomma chilensis or Homeomma sp. chilensis.

An adorable dwarf species of tarantula with a temperament to match. This is a great beginners tarantula that grows around the 8 or 9cm mark. These are so timid that we've read reports where keepers offer injured feeder prey so that the Chilean flame would not be frightened off.

They are mostly black, except for the bright orange/red tuft of hair/setae where the abdomen meets the carapace. The slings of this species are quite cute looking too, with a light brown carapace, almost transparent legs and little white abdomens. They grow pretty slowly and gain little in size between molts. These are fossorial tarantulas in nature, building shallow webbed burrows beneath rocks or broken logs. In captivity they seem to feel comfortable enough staying out in the open, so design your enclosures based on your specific specimen.

They are quite curious and will often wander up and out of their enclosures during maintenance, or might even choose to climb on to you while you work. They rarely show any skittish or defensive behaviour at all, but as always, get to know your own specimen.

It's said that in nature, their burrows are found quite close to each other, even under the same rock. Perhaps some experiments with communal setups should be tested? Hmmm, interesting.

This is currently quite an expensive tarantula due to it's rarity, but breeding efforts are slowly bringing their numbers up and values down, meaning we should see more of them in the hobby soon.

Mature Female

SCIENTIFIC NAME	Hysterocrates gigas
COMMON NAMES	Cameroon Red Baboon

ORIGIN   Cameroon, Congo, Gabon, Guinea

TYPE	TEMPERAMENT
Old World, Fossorial, Swimmer, Communal	Defensive, may stridulate fangs (hiss)

LIFESPAN	ADULT SIZE	GROWTH RATE
Females (10 to 12 years) | Males (2 to 4 years)	15cm to 16cm	Fast

SUGGESTED ENCLOSURE TEMPERATURES	SUGGESTED ENCLOSURE HUMIDITY
Winter (20 to 22°C) | Summer (24 to 26°C)	60% to 80%

BASIC ENCLOSURE REQUIREMENTS: Fossorial set-up with 15cm to 20cm of substrate with a buried shelter or starting burrow and a large water dish.

Hysterocrates gigas is a large baboon spider originating over quite a few territories across Africa. As usual with African baboon species, they aren't exactly what you could call friendly and are not to be trifled with. Just like Pelinobius muticus – The King Baboon Spider, the Cameroon Red Baboon Spider will also strike a pose, threat pose that is, and may even stridulate (hiss) using the special bristles between it's fangs. They're a stunning deep chocolate brown with lighter velvet brown tones over most their bodies and legs. On full grown adults, pink/red can be seen in the striping on their patella/knees similar to Theraphosa stirmi that even shines through on the carapace. Due to the ease of breeding this species, it's sadly undervalued but make a fantastic addition to any collection, especially if you're looking to add a baboon spider to your collection.

They're busy bodies, often bulldozing and redecorating their enclosures until it's just the way they want it. They also eat really well and grow quite fast. A behaviour of the Cameroon Red Baboon that is being tested by many hobbyists is it's ability to swim, and even catch prey under water. Keep in mind that tarantulas can't see very well, so don't expect them to chase after small fish with much success. However, if you can provide them with a decent size fish or frog, there is a good chance it will eventually be snatched up for lunch. Hobbyists are trying all sorts of enclosure configurations to put it's abilities to the test, from basic terrariums to full living paludariums. The Cameroon Red Baboon is also known to be a very good candidate for communal set-ups and many hobbyists report maintaining communal set-ups with success.

Breeding this species is relatively easy and females make great moms. Mating is an intense affair, females will rush up to males and lift their abdomens vertically. Males somehow articulate their pedipalps vertically as well and once an insert is made, he will forcefully pull the female's abdomen down and towards him. At this point he should be protected in case the female decides to grab him. Egg sacs are produced a few months later and contain anywhere from 150 to 250 eggs which can be left with the female to care for until her spiderlings start leaving the shelter. If you choose to remove and incubate the eggs manually, this can be done from about week 3 or 4.

Mature Female

SCIENTIFIC NAME	Lampropelma nigerrimum
COMMON NAMES	Sangihe Island Black, Sangihe Black

ORIGIN   Sangihe Island, Indonesia

TYPE
Old World, Semi-Arboreal

TEMPERAMENT
Defensive and fast

LIFESPAN	ADULT SIZE	GROWTH RATE
Females (12 to 15 years) | Males (3 to 4 years)	16cm to 18cm	Fast

SUGGESTED ENCLOSURE TEMPERATURES
Winter (22 to 24°C) | Summer (26 to 28°C)

SUGGESTED ENCLOSURE HUMIDITY
70% to 80%

BASIC ENCLOSURE REQUIREMENTS: Terrestrial set-up with 5cm to 10cm of substrate with vertical structures like hollow bamboo or cork bark and a water dish.

The Sangihe Island Black tarantula is a large black arboreal tarantula with feathery feet/ tarsi, which unfortunately spends very little time out in the open. In captivity, they seem to prefer a hollow vertical shelter like tubular cork bark or bamboo which reaches below the substrate and they seldom venture out except when hunting for prey. When they do appear, they are stunning black beauties to behold, especially as full-grown adults. Youngsters display sheens of purple as they grow but become primarily black once they reach adulthood. They can be nervous and skittish when disturbed and care should be taken when working with them from sling to adult because they move with extreme speed. A bite from an adult female will definitely be significantly painful not only due to the size of their fangs but also their potent old-world venom.

Mature Male

Breeding this species is relatively easy but if the female is not 100% happy with her surroundings she may destroy or eat her eggs sac. Females can be quite tolerant of males (which look quite different as seen on the right) and we've often allowed males to co-habit with females for a few days but not too long or he will become a meal if she gets tired of his presence. You will know when the male is making an attempt to mate because he will tap the enclosure pretty hard with three to four loud taps in a row, rather than lots of smaller taps as seen in many tarantulas. The males tend to be scaredy-cats and don't easily engage a female, leading her around the enclosure for hours until she gets bored and goes back to her shelter. This can also lead to her becoming frustrated and attacking so we suggest making sure at least one mating is successful before leaving him with the female for any extended period of time.

If mating is successful, the female will usually lay an egg sac quite a few months later which can be removed immediately to avoid any risk of it being destroyed, or 4 to 5 weeks later if you choose to leave it with mom for longer. You can expect an egg sac to contain anywhere from 80 to 150 eggs

Juvenile Female

SCIENTIFIC NAME	Lasiodora parahybana
COMMON NAMES	Salmon Pink Bird-Eater

ORIGIN Brazil

TYPE	TEMPERAMENT
New World, Terrestrial	Bold, may flick urticating bristles

LIFESPAN	ADULT SIZE	GROWTH RATE
Females (15 to 20 years)	Males (3 to 4 years)	25cm to 28cm	Medium to Fast

SUGGESTED ENCLOSURE TEMPERATURES	SUGGESTED ENCLOSURE HUMIDITY
Winter (22 to 24°C)	Summer (24 to 28°C)	60% to 80%

BASIC ENCLOSURE REQUIREMENTS: Terrestrial set-up with 5cm to 10cm of substrate, lots of space for larger specimens, a shelter and a water dish.

Looking for something big? Really big? The Salmon Pink Bird-Eater tarantula ranks among the worlds heavy-weights when it comes to size. They are only trumped in adult size by the Theraphosa genus, which include Theraphosa blondi (Goliath Bird-Eater), Theraphosa apohpysis (Pink Foot Goliath Bird-Eater) and Theraphosa stirmi (Burgundy Goliath Bird-Eater) tarantulas, which are far more rare and much more expensive.

Starting at a few millimeters as a spiderling they grow up to 25cm (10 inches) and more as adults. This is a true giant when it comes to tarantulas, they can be a bit skittish and a bit nervous when young, but usually become very timid and mellow as they age. They tend to get quite slow and patient at full grown sizes, making them an attractive species to consider handling but it's essential that you get to know your specific specimen because some of them can be quite feisty. Also, with females getting so large and heavy, great care should be taken if attempting handling because any significant fall will potentially injure or cause fatal internal damage to your tarantula. They are otherwise hardy spiders, require very little in terms of enclosure requirements and are generally a pleasure to keep and work with.

Juvenile Female

Breeding this species is very easy but males should always be protected during mating as females are very prone to attacking and eating males. Egg sacs are large and may contain upward of 800 tiny eggs which can be manually incubated from about week 5. Hobbyists that breed the Salmon Pink for fun or simply because it's easy are guilty of flooding the hobby with far too many of this species, which is why they are so cheap and always in over-supply. They are often given away for free. Beware, they are also used by scammers claiming to be selling Goliath Bird-Eaters (Theraphosa species), but their slings looks completely different and a beginner or uncertain buyer should always ask an expert before buying any Theraphosa spiderlings, especially if being sold online or in classified listings.

Mature Female

Monocentropus balfouri

Socotra Island Blue Baboon Spider / Tarantula

ORIGIN Socotra island, Yemen

TYPE
Old World, Terrestrial, Heavy webber, Communal

TEMPERAMENT
Bold but nervous, can be defensive

LIFESPAN
Females (10 to 15 years) | Males (2 to 4 years)

ADULT SIZE
11cm to 12cm

GROWTH RATE
Medium

SUGGESTED ENCLOSURE TEMPERATURES
Winter (24 to 26°C) | Summer (26 to 28°C)

SUGGESTED ENCLOSURE HUMIDITY
40% to 50%

BASIC ENCLOSURE REQUIREMENTS: Terrestrial set-up with 10cm to 15cm of substrate, lots of structure to anchor webbing, a shelter and a water dish.

Rated by many enthusiasts to be the most beautiful tarantula of all, Monocentropus balfouri is a special and beautiful baboon spider. Almost wiped out from their home habitat on the island of Socotra, numbers now thrive around the world thanks to the tarantula hobby.

Truly a beautiful tarantula to behold. A creamy light-brown abdomen and femurs are contrasted by dark blue setae/hair on the legs from the patella/knees down to their feet/tarsi. The carapace has light metallic blue hues all over it finished with a creamy fringe around it's perimeter. At 12cm, they aren't the biggest tarantulas but due to their unique appearance and heavy webbing characteristics they're a must-have for any collection, especially with Monocentropus balfouri being one of few species that are truly capable of co-habitation and will thrive in a communal setting.

Provide lots of space and structure in their communal enclosures and you'll be treated to a webbed wonderland of tarantulas. From sling to adult, their temperament is surprisingly mellow for an old world species and have a peaceful demeanor overall, especially with each other. A unique observation is that females even care for slings from a different mother and can all stay with mom until they have no choice but to move out due to a lack of space. Although some cannibalism occurs, they are generally very tolerant of each other and not only share burrows, but food as well.

Calm as they are, they're capable of break-neck speeds and will throw a threat-pose if startled or provoked and we all know what comes after that. It's still a baboon spider and will defend itself properly if not respected.

This species prefers a dry environment over all, including when breeding. Mating is a fairly relaxed affair and females rarely exhibit any aggression towards males, but will eat a male if left in a single female's enclosure for too long. In a communal setting, males fare much better. Monocentropus balfouri will lay a fixed egg sac containing anywhere from 100 to 250 eggs. Females make great mothers and it's suggested that spiderlings are left with the mothers until at least third or fourth instar (molt) to get a good healthy start at life.

Mature Female

SCIENTIFIC NAME	# Neoholothele incei NCF
COMMON NAMES	Trinidad Olive NCF, Bumble Bee Tarantula NCF: Normal Colour Form

ORIGIN Trinidad / Venezuela

TYPE
New World, Fossorial, Webber, Dwarf Species, Communal

TEMPERAMENT
Nervous, fast moving

LIFESPAN
Females (6 to 7 years) | Males (1 to 2 years)

ADULT SIZE
5cm to 7cm

GROWTH RATE
Fast

SUGGESTED ENCLOSURE TEMPERATURES
Winter (22 to 25°C) | Summer (25 to 28°C)

SUGGESTED ENCLOSURE HUMIDITY
60% to 70%

BASIC ENCLOSURE REQUIREMENTS: Fossorial set-up with 10cm to 15cm of substrate, lots of structure to anchor webbing, a shelter and a water dish.

One of the smaller species in the hobby, growing no larger than 7cm and capable of being kept in a communal set-up due to their relative tolerance for one another. They're an attractive species with a black and gold star-burst on the carapace, gold highlights on it's legs and a clear "Bee" pattern on the abdomen, giving it the nickname "Bumble Bee". Very skittish and extremely quick for their size, they can be a handful during feeding or when enclosure maintenance is required. It's normal to have one of these on your back because they bolt at incredible pace and cover an amazing amount of ground in a very short time.

Mostly harmless, they will rarely show any aggression or defensive qualities, however every specimen is different so as always get to know yours. To our knowledge there are very few bite reports from this species, the few that were reported only described burning at the site of a bite.

The Trinidad Olive will produce copious amounts of webbing in and around it's home, eventually covering everything in sight, so an enclosure with a decent amount of structure in the form of small branches and drift wood is a good idea. We've bred and raised these easily and successfully as single spiders and as communal colonies. Cannibalism happens from time to time, but very rarely if enough space and structure is provided.

Males should be protected during mating because we've seen females launch sudden snack-attacks when mating comes to a close. Females are otherwise tolerant of males during mating, allowing him to make multiple inserts with both pedipalps until he is satisfied that his work is done. Depending on the size of the female, egg sacs are about 2 to 3cm in size and carry approximately 50 to 100 eggs. They are great mothers if environmental conditions are maintained so you can either leave the egg sac with mom full term or pull it away for manual incubation after about 4 weeks after laying.

Mature Female

Neoholothele incei GCF

SCIENTIFIC NAME	Neoholothele incei GCF
COMMON NAMES	Trinidad Olive GCF, Trinidad Gold Olive GCF: Gold Colour Form

ORIGIN Trinidad / Venezuela

TYPE
New World, Fossorial, Webber, Dwarf Species, Communal

TEMPERAMENT
Nervous, fast moving

LIFESPAN
Females (6 to 7 years) | Males (1 to 2 years)

ADULT SIZE
5cm to 7cm

GROWTH RATE
Fast

SUGGESTED ENCLOSURE TEMPERATURES
Winter (22 to 25°C) | Summer (25 to 28°C)

SUGGESTED ENCLOSURE HUMIDITY
60% to 70%

BASIC ENCLOSURE REQUIREMENTS: Fossorial set-up with 10cm to 15cm of substrate, lots of structure to anchor webbing, a shelter and a water dish.

When it comes to looks, size is the only thing in common between the Neoholothele incei (NCF) and Neoholothele incei (GCF). The Trinidad "Gold" Olive is absolutely adorable with golden-pink colouring over it's entire body. It still retains the "Bumble Bee" pattern like the NCF, but it's only visible under good lighting.

Genetically, the NCF and GCF are the same species, except that a gold colour form gene has been discovered through breeding and can now be selectively bred for. For a simple explanation, the normal colour genes are dominant and the gold genes are recessive, meaning that mating an NCF parent with a GCF parent should always result in 100% NCF offspring. However, if the NCF parent also carries the recessive GCF gene (weather by luck or by a previous breeding project) and is mated with a GCF specimen, both NCF and GCF offspring will be produced in the same hatch (roughly 25% will be GCF) and offspring will carry the recessive GCF gene from there on.

Mature Male

NCF mated with NCF should produce 100% NCF offspring and GCF mated with GCF should produce 100% GCF offspring.

Other than being different in colour, their temperament, behaviours and traits are much like their NCF siblings, they're just as fast, web like crazy and also tolerate each other in a spacious communal set-up. Breeding is also exactly the same as the NCF Trinidad Olive. They breed quite easily and no special equipments are necessary except their regular environmental conditions.

The mature female on the adjacent page was mated with the mature male pictured here and we're waiting and hoping for the female to lay an egg sac at the time of this writing.

Juvenile Female

SCIENTIFIC NAME # Nhandu chromatus

COMMON NAMES Brazilian Red & White, White Striped Bird-Eater

ORIGIN   Brazil / Paraguay

TYPE
New World, Terrestrial

TEMPERAMENT
Nervous, may flick urticating bristles

LIFESPAN
Females (12 to 15 years) | Males (3 to 4 years)

ADULT SIZE   GROWTH RATE
16cm to 17cm   Medium to Fast

SUGGESTED ENCLOSURE TEMPERATURES
Winter (20 to 24°C) | Summer (24 to 28°C)

SUGGESTED ENCLOSURE HUMIDITY
60% to 80%

BASIC ENCLOSURE REQUIREMENTS: Terrestrial set-up with 10cm to 15cm of substrate, a shelter and a water dish.

The best bang for buck in the hobby.

This is generally an inexpensive tarantula with striking colours, it grows to be a whopping 16cm and more, eats like crazy and to top it off, it's bold and spends a lot of it's time in the open. It ticks all the boxes. Although this species is a bit skittish and feisty, it's striking colouration and cheeky attitude make it a very interesting tarantula for beginners, but handling is not recommended.

They will construct holes and shallow burrows as slings and juveniles, but as adults Nhandu chromatus grow to be quite large and spends a lot of time out in the open, making them a great display specimen as well. They are great eaters with explosive feeding responses, more than willing to grab more than one feeder item at a time. This is usually followed by some pretty elaborate happy dances as well.

Any significant disturbance usually makes this tarantula bolt for cover, especially when younger. Contact or continued provocation often results in urticating bristles being flicked at you. You may even see a raised abdomen and eventually a threat pose if you annoy it enough. However it will seldom follow through with it's threats and will probably run for cover before trying to bite. Don't push your luck though, all tarantulas will bite if pushed far enough. Get to know your individual specimens.

Breeding this species is very easy and unfortunately often leads to over supply in tarantula communities. The result being that they have become very low in value. Regardless, they are gorgeous as full-grown specimens and you will find even the most experienced hobbyists will have one of these hiding somewhere in their collection.

Mature males are large and lanky, usually escaping a mating attempt unharmed but should be guarded just to be safe. Females produce egg sacs without any special conditions and you can expect anywhere upwards of 500 eggs to be produced. The sac can be manually incubated from about week 5 from laying.

Mature Female

Nhandu coloratovillosus

Brazilian Black & White, Bombardier Tarantula

ORIGIN Brazil / Paraguay

TYPE
New World, Terrestrial

TEMPERAMENT
Nervous, can be defensive

LIFESPAN
Females (12 to 15 years) | Males (3 to 4 years)

ADULT SIZE
15cm to 16cm

GROWTH RATE
Medium to Fast

SUGGESTED ENCLOSURE TEMPERATURES
Winter (22 to 24°C) | Summer (26 to 28°C)

SUGGESTED ENCLOSURE HUMIDITY
60% to 80%

BASIC ENCLOSURE REQUIREMENTS: Terrestrial set-up with 10cm to 15cm of substrate, a shelter and a water dish.

Nhandu coloratovillosus is another great looking tarantula for your collection. Black and cream striped legs, a dark carapace and dark abdomen covered in long reddish setae/hair make this tarantula look fluffy and adorable! Don't be fooled though, their temperament varies widely from specimen to specimen and also from one moment to the next.

The female specimen photographed here was very skittish and nervous when we removed her from her enclosure to photograph, then suddenly sat still and didn't show any further nervous behaviour for the next 10 minutes as we positioned her for different photos.

When we tried to move her back to her enclosure, she suddenly flared up in a threat pose and attempted to bite. We always try to impress on all hobbyists that they should get to know their specific specimens before getting too comfortable with them.

Nhandu coloratovillosus grows quite large and although they bolt for cover when disturbed, they will soon emerge again for all to see, making them great for display. They're incredible eaters and will happily grab more than one prey item at a time. Our specimen was a guts and continued eating well in to pre-molt.

They grow quite quickly, gaining significant size between molts and their adult colours become visible from quite young. Unfortunately, much like it's cousin Nhandu chromatus, they barely web, except when a molt is due or when laying eggs.

This species is also quite easy to breed and no special preparation or requirements are necessary to encourage the female to produce an egg sac. With the feisty nature of the female, make sure to protect males during mating. If mating is successful, you can expect an egg sac to contain upward of 200 eggs.

Mature Female

SCIENTIFIC NAME	Nhandu tripepii
COMMON NAMES	Brazilian Giant Blonde, Strawberry Blonde Tarantula

ORIGIN Para, Brazil

TYPE
New World, Terrestrial, Opportunistic Burrower

TEMPERAMENT
Nervous, may flick urticating bristles

LIFESPAN
Females (12 to 15 years) | Males (4 to 5 years)

ADULT SIZE
16cm to 17cm

GROWTH RATE
Medium to Fast

SUGGESTED ENCLOSURE TEMPERATURES
Winter (22 to 24°C) | Summer (24 to 28°C)

SUGGESTED ENCLOSURE HUMIDITY
60% to 80%

BASIC ENCLOSURE REQUIREMENTS: Terrestrial set-up with 10cm to 15cm of substrate, a shelter and a water dish.

One of the bushiest bird spiders in the business. Nhandu tripepii is a large terrestrial tarantula with long pinkish setae/hairs all over it's body, giving it an overall strawberry-blonde appearance. They have a nervous and skittish temperament and are even worse in bright light. You might find your Brazilian Giant Blonde acting very unhappy and restless if it's enclosure is kept in a bright space.

Known to burrow and hide when younger, the Brazilian Blonde grows quickly, reaching roughly 17cm at full size. A full grown female is impressive in person, which is a bonus because they are bold and stay out in the open as they grow larger, making them a great and big display tarantula. They have a voracious appetite, almost every prey item offered to them will be met with significant force.

Nhandu tripepii are generally very easy going when comfortable in their enclosures and can be active both day and night. They can really be busy bodies, investigating their enclosures for hours, just as much as they can stand in one place for what seems to be forever.

Impressive and super fluffy, this is a great addition to your collection especially since they don't fetch very high prices, making them good value for money too.

This species is also quite easy to breed and no special preparation or requirements are necessary to encourage the female to produce an egg sac. Make sure to protect males during mating even though mating commonly takes place without any vicious behaviour.

If mating is successful, you can expect an egg sac to contain anywhere from 600 to 1000 eggs, maybe even more. No small task and will require hard work to look after all these slings once they hatch, so be prepared. The egg sac can be pulled away from the female for manual incubation from about the 4th or 5th week after laying.

Mature Female

SCIENTIFIC NAME	Omothymus violaceopes
COMMON NAMES	Singapore Blue

ORIGIN Malaysia / Singapore

TYPE
Old World, Arboreal

TEMPERAMENT
Nervous, defensive and fast moving

LIFESPAN
Females (12 to 15 years) | Males (3 to 4 years)

ADULT SIZE
19cm to 21cm

GROWTH RATE
Fast

SUGGESTED ENCLOSURE TEMPERATURES
Winter (22 to 24°C) | Summer (26 to 28°C)

SUGGESTED ENCLOSURE HUMIDITY
60% to 80%

BASIC ENCLOSURE REQUIREMENTS: Arboreal setup with 10cm to 15cm of substrate, a vertical shelter like hollow cork bark or bamboo and a water dish.

Another blue beauty in the world of Tarantulas. The Singapore Blue (previously described under the Lampropelma genus) is an Old World arboreal tarantula that grows fast and grows large. It has a relatively small body compared to it's long outstretched and feathery blue legs, which they use to move with considerable speed. They are generally quite shy and spend a lot of time in their arboreal shelters, but we have seen that once they become accustomed to the room they're kept in, they slowly get bolder and braver and can be seen out and about quite often, only retreating with a disturbance. From sling to adult, they are voracious feeders and almost never turn down a meal which probably adds to why they grow so fast. Try to avoid over-feeding so you get to enjoy your specimen as long as possible.

This is an Old World species and should be respected as such. Adults have a painful bite simply due to the sheer size of their fangs, which with some added Old World Venom is going to ruin your day completely, so always take care when working with your Singapore Blue. They like to live in tubular shelters that reach from the upper areas of the enclosure down below the substrate which they may excavate right to the bottom.

Breeding this species is a challenge because females can be unreliable in caring for their eggs. Males are dull and scrawny compared to females but generally get the mating job done quite effectively. During mating, the male will lure the female away from her shelter and mate on a vertical surface he finds suitable. Keep mated females at temperatures around 26°C with good ventilation and humidity around 70 to 80%.

As mentioned, females can be a bit unpredictable when it comes to caring for their egg sacs, so breeding attempts are not always successful. It's up to you to decide if you will leave the sac with mom or remove it as soon as possible. You can expect between 60 and 120 eggs.

Mature Female

SCIENTIFIC NAME	Pamphobeteus sp. Machala
COMMON NAMES	Colombian Purple Bloom, Purple Bloom, Purple Starburst

ORIGIN   Machala, Ecuador

TYPE	TEMPERAMENT
New World, Terrestrial	Bold, nervous

LIFESPAN	ADULT SIZE	GROWTH RATE
Females (18 to 20 years) | Males (3 to 4 years)	18cm to 20cm	Medium to Fast

SUGGESTED ENCLOSURE TEMPERATURES	SUGGESTED ENCLOSURE HUMIDITY
Winter (20 to 24°C) | Summer (24 to 28°C)	60% to 80%

BASIC ENCLOSURE REQUIREMENTS: Terrestrial set-up with 5cm to 10cm of substrate, a large shelter and a water dish.

If it's a Pamphobeteus, it's big, eats well and grows fast. Sought after in the hobby for their sheer size as adults, Pamphobeteus species are only trumped in size by the Theraphosa genus of giants. Starting out as large spiderlings, they eat heartily and grow fast. They soon become juveniles, losing the colourful red/orange and black "Christmas Tree" pattern visible on their abdomens as slings. An adult female is impressive to see in person. With good lighting, purple and burgundy hues can just barely be seen on an adult female. But mature males are a different story, displaying an absolutely stunning amount of lavender and metallic purples on their legs with a huge purple starburst pattern on their carapace, giving the "Purple Bloom" it's common name.

These tarantulas make great display pieces, they don't scare easily and are more than willing to sit out in the open. They have a bold disposition and although they will flee or be nervous at times, they also tend to be curious and will grab your maintenance tools from you if you aren't paying attention. They have great appetites and will rarely pass up the chance for a meal unless in pre-molt or if they've eaten far too much already. For the most part, they are generally pretty laid back and amazing giants to own.

Mature Male

This species can be difficult to breed, females are unpredictable and sensitive to changes in their environment. If conditions aren't perfect or they change suddenly, females are prone to destroy or consume their egg sacs. They also seem to require a warm dry environment that becomes wet by a rainy season, drying out slowly again to trigger females in to laying an egg sac. Humidity should be around 70 to 80% and the temperature around 26 to 28°C. If you're lucky and she produces an egg sac, it can be removed from the female within a few days for manual incubation, or 5 weeks after laying if you choose. Expect around 100 to 150 large eggs.

Mature Female

SCIENTIFIC NAME	Pamphobeteus ultramarinus
COMMON NAMES	Ecuador Bird Eater, Ecuadorian Bird Eater

ORIGIN Andean regions of Colombia, Ecuador, and Peru

TYPE
New World, Terrestrial, Opportunistic Burrower

TEMPERAMENT
Bold, nervous

LIFESPAN
Females (18 to 20 years) | Males (3 to 4 years)

ADULT SIZE
18cm to 20cm

GROWTH RATE
Medium to Fast

SUGGESTED ENCLOSURE TEMPERATURES
Winter (20 to 24°C) | Summer (24 to 28°C)

SUGGESTED ENCLOSURE HUMIDITY
70% to 80%

BASIC ENCLOSURE REQUIREMENTS: Terrestrial set-up with 5cm to 10cm of substrate, a large shelter and a water dish.

The awesome appearance and size of the Ecuadorian Bird-Eater, means you can't help but want one of these for your collection. A large, beautiful new world species with jet blacks, browns and metallic hues of blue and purple seen over it's body, and those are the girls.

As with Pamphobeteus sp. Machala, mature males of this species are far more colourful than females after their ultimate molt, sadly we did not find a specimen to photograph for this publication. Slings have pinkish-orange abdomens displaying a "Christmas Tree" pattern that eventually fades as the spider grows.

Many Pamphobeteus species are found in the Andean regions of Colombia, Ecuador, and Peru. Pamphobeteus ultramarinus is found east of the Andean region along with Pamphobeteus antinous, Pamphobeteus petersi and the true Pamphobeteus nigricolor. Tena, Ecuador where Pamphobeteus ultramarinus is found, is surrounded by rain forest with a cooler and drier climate than is found in the Amazon basin. Moisture still remains a requirement with this species so good airflow and high humidity should be provided. Ensuring constant access to water in the form of a nice large water dish is also a good idea.

Spiderlings are hardy, eat well, grow fast and do very well at room temperatures. Like the other Pamphobeteus species, this species is bold and happy to bask out in the open, only scurrying away with a significant disturbance. They are also voracious eaters and prey items will regularly be met with healthy helpings of crunchy vigor. Make sure to supply a fair amount of substrate in case your tarantula decides it wants to do some burrowing.

Males should always be protected when mating Pamphobeteus species because females can be unpredictable. The same applies when it comes to laying eggs. A dry environment introduced to a rainy season which slowly dries out and cools again seems to assist in triggering females to produce an egg sac. You can consider removing the egg sac for manual incubation immediately or you can risk leaving it with the mother full term in case she's a good mom. You can expect anywhere between 120 to 180 eggs.

Mature Female

SCIENTIFIC NAME	# Poecilotheria metallica
COMMON NAMES	Sapphire Ornamental

ORIGIN   Nallamala Forest, India

TYPE
Old World, Arboreal

TEMPERAMENT
Nervous to defensive

LIFESPAN
Females (10 to 12 years) | Males (2 to 3 years)

ADULT SIZE
14cm to 15cm

GROWTH RATE
Fast

SUGGESTED ENCLOSURE TEMPERATURES
Winter (22 to 24°C) | Summer (26 to 28°C)

SUGGESTED ENCLOSURE HUMIDITY
70% to 80%

BASIC ENCLOSURE REQUIREMENTS: Arboreal set-up with 10cm to 15cm of substrate, a vertical shelter like hollow cork bark or bamboo and a water dish.

The Sapphire Ornamental remains one of the most sought-after tarantula species in the world. Starting as boring gray-ish slings, females mature in to a flurry of blues, whites and yellows that keep your eyes glued. They lose some of their vibrant colours with age and some blue areas become dark gray or even black. Mature males are smaller and duller than females and don't possess tibial hooks/spurs at maturity. Poecilotheria live behind bark and in crevices of large trees in the wild, so try provide them with vertical structure that dives in to a decent depth of substrate. We've seen too many enclosures with one bushy plastic plant in the middle of the enclosure which the poor tarantula can't walk on and is forced to live up against the glass with no shelter. They prefer vertical pieces of wood or cork bark propped up in a corner of an enclosure with even more wide branches to walk across.

They have the best temperament of all Poecilotheria, known to hunker down and wait for danger to pass or possibly run, rather than throw a threat pose or show aggression. This doesn't mean they're not capable of getting defensive or delivering a painful bite. Always respect them and practice caution, their bite is significantly unpleasant. Although docile as pokies go, these tarantulas move invisibly fast when they decide to run for it, so extreme care is necessary.

During mating, females are usually tolerant of males, but if you see any aggression from the female, remove

Mature Male

the male and try again later or he may be destroyed. Breeding this species is somewhat difficult. A gravid female will grow a large abdomen full of eggs, which is a good sign, but she may not lay at all. Increased heat coupled with humidity above 80% and perfect darkness seem to assist in triggering females to produce egg sacs. The sac can be removed for manual incubation 5 weeks after laying or immediately as females can be unpredictable. Expect anywhere between 80 to 150 eggs.

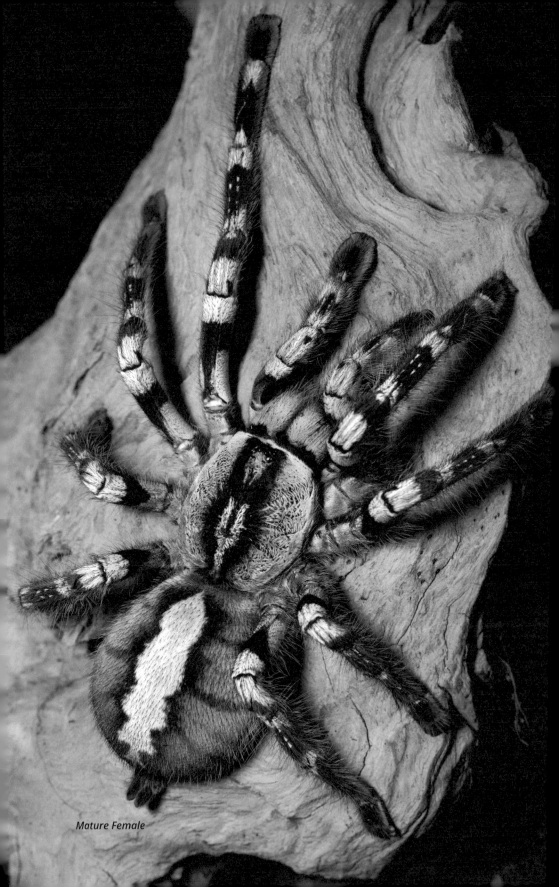

Mature Female

SCIENTIFIC NAME	Poecilotheria regalis
COMMON NAMES	Indian Ornamental, Regal Parachute Spider

ORIGIN   Various locations in India

TYPE
Old World, Arboreal

TEMPERAMENT
Defensive and aggressive if provoked

LIFESPAN
Females (10 to 12 years) | Males (2 to 3 years)

ADULT SIZE
17cm to 18cm

GROWTH RATE
Fast

SUGGESTED ENCLOSURE TEMPERATURES
Winter (22 to 24°C) | Summer (26 to 28°C)

SUGGESTED ENCLOSURE HUMIDITY
70% to 80%

BASIC ENCLOSURE REQUIREMENTS: Arboreal set-up with 10cm to 15cm of substrate, a vertical shelter like hollow cork bark or bamboo and a water dish.

A hobby favourite that grows large and is a gorgeous sight. Most Poecilotheria or "Pokies" develop a beautiful contrast of blacks, browns and creamy white colours on the upper sides of their bodies. The undersides are a mix of black, gray and white banding on most of the Pokies, but with P. regalis and a few others, those colours are met with bright yellow banding as well. A clear warning to predators or careless hobbyists. P. regalis and P. rajaei are also easily identified apart from other Pokies by a creamy-pink band which crosses the underside of their abdomens between both sets of book lungs, this is visible on both males and females through to maturity.

The venom of P. regalis is potent and it will gladly deliver a nasty bite if provoked. Bites are very painful, not only due to the size of their fangs, but their venom is well reported as being significantly powerful, causing intense burning likened to dipping your arm in boiling oil, even causing blistering skin at the site of the bite. Medication may be required just to deal with the pain. Random and painful cramping is also to be expected in the areas of the bite but also in other muscles of the body for up to 6 months in some cases. Pokies are serious old world tarantulas and are not for beginners or inexperienced hobbyists.

Breeding P. regalis is not too difficult. Mating should be conducted in a larger mating arena as males will attempt to lead the female away from her enclosure until he feels safe to engage her. Mating goes ahead quite quickly and males will bolt for cover the instant an insertion is made, do your best to keep him safe from the female or from falling. A cool wet period of 22°C warmed slowly to around 28°C with high humidity seems to encourage females to produce an egg sac. Egg sacs can be pulled away from the female at about 4 weeks for manual incubation if you choose, this is recommended as Pokies are known to eat their egg sacs when they don't feel things are perfect. You can expect in the region of 100 to 200 eggs.

Mature Female

SCIENTIFIC NAME	Poecilotheria rufilata
COMMON NAMES	Red Slate Ornamental, Rufus Parachute Spider

ORIGIN   South-Western Ghats, India

TYPE	TEMPERAMENT
Old World, Arboreal	Defensive and aggressive if provoked

LIFESPAN	ADULT SIZE	GROWTH RATE
Females (10 to 12 years)	Males (2 to 3 years)	18cm to 22cm	Fast

SUGGESTED ENCLOSURE TEMPERATURES	SUGGESTED ENCLOSURE HUMIDITY
Winter (22 to 24°C)	Summer (26 to 28°C)	60% to 70%

BASIC ENCLOSURE REQUIREMENTS: Arboreal set-up with 10cm to 15cm of substrate, a vertical shelter like hollow cork bark or bamboo and a water dish.

The Red Slate Ornamental is quite a special looking Poecilotheria species. Their bodies are mostly a deep olive colour with black and rich yellow accents, covered with pale red setae/hairs. They have light yellow banding under their legs, getting duller from the front to the back legs. They move incredibly fast from sling to adult and grow at a quick pace. They're also one of the largest pokies, reaching up to 22cm in total diagonal leg-span. A full grown female is beautiful to see in person. Sadly, due to low numbers and deforestation, these are considered endangered but are still seen in the hobby thanks to breeders. The venom of P. rufilata is expected to be as potent as other pokies and it will gladly deliver a nasty bite if provoked. Bites are very painful, not only due to the size of their fangs, but their venom is also reported as being significantly powerful, causing intense burning likened to dipping your arm in boiling oil, even causing blistering skin at the site of the bite. Medication may be required just to deal with the pain. Random and painful cramping is also to be expected in the areas of the bite but also in other muscles of the body for up to 6 months in some cases. Pokies are serious old world tarantulas and are not for beginners or inexperienced hobbyists.

Breeding P. rufilata should be attempted the same as other pokies. Mating should be conducted in a larger mating arena, Poecilotheria males usually lead the female away from her enclosure until feeling safe to engage her. Mating goes ahead quite quickly and males will bolt for cover the instant an insertion is made, do your best to keep him safe from the female or from falling. A cool wet period of 22°C warmed slowly to around 28°C with high humidity seems to encourage females to produce an egg sac. Egg sacs can be pulled away from the female at about 4 weeks for manual incubation if you choose, this is recommended as Pokies are known to eat their egg sacs when they don't feel things are perfect. You can expect in the region of 80 to 150 eggs.

Mature Female

Poecilotheria hanumavilasumica

Rameshwaram Ornamental

ORIGIN   Island of Rameshwaram / Ramanthapuram district, Southern India

TYPE	TEMPERAMENT	
Old World, Arboreal	Defensive and aggressive if provoked	

LIFESPAN	ADULT SIZE	GROWTH RATE
Females (10 to 12 years) | Males (2 to 3 years)	16cm to 18cm	Fast

SUGGESTED ENCLOSURE TEMPERATURES	SUGGESTED ENCLOSURE HUMIDITY
Winter (22 to 24°C) | Summer (26 to 28°C)	70% to 80%

BASIC ENCLOSURE REQUIREMENTS: Arboreal set-up with 10cm to 15cm of substrate, a vertical shelter like hollow cork bark or bamboo and a water dish.

The Rameshwaram Ornamental is considered to be critically endangered. First identified in 2004, they're only found in specific areas between Mannar, Sri Lanka and Mandapam, India, including Rameshwaram island. They're similar in appearance to Poecilotheria fasciata – Sri Lankan Ornamentals, but variances in colour bands on the underside of P. hanumavilasumica clearly separate the two. Broader yellow bands on the femurs of legs one and two and a continuous yellow band on leg 4 as opposed to a segmented band on P. fasciata are visible. The spermatheca organ is also different to P. fasciata, a clear identifier.

The venom of P. hanumavilasumica is expected to be as potent as all other pokies and it will gladly deliver a nasty bite if provoked. Bites are very painful, not only due to the size of their fangs, but their venom is well reported as being significantly powerful. Causing intense burning likened to dipping your arm in boiling oil, even causing blistering skin at the site of the bite. Medication may be required for a careless or unlucky hobbyist just to deal with the pain. Random and painful cramping is also to be expected in the areas of the bite but also in other muscles of the body for up to 6 months in some cases. Pokies are serious old world tarantulas and are not for beginners or inexperienced hobbyists.

Breeding P. hanumavilasumica should be attempted the same as other pokies. Mating should be conducted in a larger mating arena, Poecilotheria males will usually lead the female away from her enclosure until he feels safe to engage her. Mating goes ahead quite quickly, the males will bolt for cover the instant an insertion is made, do your best to keep him safe from the female or from falling. A cool wet period of 22°C warmed slowly to around 28°C with high humidity seems to encourage females to produce an egg sac. Egg sacs can be pulled away from the female at about 4 weeks for manual incubation if you choose, this is recommended as Pokies are known to eat their egg sacs when they don't feel things are perfect. You can expect in the region of 100 to 200 eggs.

Mature Female

SCIENTIFIC NAME	Poecilotheria tigrinawesseli
COMMON NAMES	Wessel's Tiger Ornamental, Anantagiri's Parachute Spider

ORIGIN   Andhra Pradesh, Eastern Ghats, India

TYPE	TEMPERAMENT
Old World, Arboreal	Defensive and aggressive if provoked

LIFESPAN	ADULT SIZE	GROWTH RATE
Females (10 to 12 years) | Males (2 to 3 years)	16cm to 18cm	Fast

SUGGESTED ENCLOSURE TEMPERATURES	SUGGESTED ENCLOSURE HUMIDITY
Winter (22 to 24°C) | Summer (26 to 28°C)	70% to 80%

BASIC ENCLOSURE REQUIREMENTS: Arboreal set-up with 10cm to 15cm of substrate, a vertical shelter like hollow cork bark or bamboo and a water dish.

Poecilotheria tigrinawesseli is another recently identified "pokie", described for the first time in 2006. They have beautiful contrasting colours on their upper body, but the banding under their legs is mostly black and white with little to no yellow seen on other pokies.

They can also be identified by the little white "T" on the carapace near the abdomen. As far as pokies go, they have stocky legs and a large robust appearance, especially a well fed adult female. You will also find metallic purple hues on the carapace and the black on all the legs almost has a deep blue or purple sheen to it.

The venom of P. tigrinawesseli is expected to be as potent as all other pokies and it will gladly deliver a nasty bite if provoked. Bites are very painful, not only due to the size of their fangs, but their venom is well reported as being significantly powerful. Causing intense burning likened to dipping your arm in boiling oil, even causing blistering skin at the site of the bite. Medication may be required for a careless or unlucky hobbyist just to deal with the pain. Random and painful cramping is also to be expected in the areas of the bite but also in other muscles of the body for up to 6 months in some cases. Pokies are serious old world tarantulas and are not for beginners or inexperienced hobbyists.

Breeding P. tigrinawesseli should be attempted the same as other pokies. Mating should be conducted in a larger mating arena, Poecilotheria males will usually lead the female away from her enclosure until he feels safe to engage her. Mating goes ahead quite quickly, the males will bolt for cover the instant an insertion is made, do your best to keep him safe from the female or from falling. A cool wet period of 22°C warmed slowly to around 28°C with high humidity seems to encourage females to produce an egg sac. Egg sacs can be pulled away from the female at about 4 weeks for manual incubation if you choose, this is recommended as Pokies are known to eat their egg sacs when they don't feel things are perfect. You can expect in the region of 60 to 120 eggs.

Mature Female

Psalmopoeus irminia

Venezuelan Sun Tiger

ORIGIN Venezuela, North-Guyana, North-Brazil, Paracaíma

TYPE	TEMPERAMENT
New World, Semi-Arboreal	Unpredictable, fast and defensive

LIFESPAN	ADULT SIZE	GROWTH RATE
Females (10 to 12 years) | Males (3 to 4 years)	13cm to 14cm	Fast

SUGGESTED ENCLOSURE TEMPERATURES	SUGGESTED ENCLOSURE HUMIDITY
Winter (20 to 22°C) | Summer (26 to 28°C)	60% to 80%

BASIC ENCLOSURE REQUIREMENTS: Arboreal set-up with 5cm to 10cm of substrate, a vertical shelter like hollow cork bark or bamboo and a water dish.

Bringing the term "exotic" to your collection. Eye-catching in black with orange accents on their legs, this new world species is more like an old world species. They have no urticating bristles and pack a nasty venom, so must be treated with respect. Their venom is medically significant and a badly placed bite would cause serious pain and discomfort. They're also very fast moving tarantulas, as slings and as adults.

Regardless, the Sun Tiger is a fantastic spider to own. They have a hearty appetite and explosive feeding responses. Building webbed burrows at the base of their vertical shelters, it's recommended to supply them with a slanted vertical shelter like a curved piece of cork bark. Their temperament is generally manageable, it's only during feeding, cleaning or maintenance that one should take care because this species is known to be unpredictable and skittish, turning to defensive and even aggressive if they are constantly provoked or feel trapped. The Sun Tiger will also jump if it thinks that's the way out. If they do happen to jump, Psalmopoeus irminia spreads it's legs to act as a parachute and skydives quite well.

During mating, a mature male placed in a mature female's enclosure will vibrate at high speed to communicate his presence. A willing female will approach with tapping and vibrations of her own. Mating goes ahead smoothly but males should be protected as mating comes to a close because females are known to grab a post-mating snack. A successfully mated female will create an egg sac a few months later containing anywhere from 80 to 200 eggs. Egg sacs can be left with the female until hatching as they make great mothers, or they can be removed for manual incubation from week 3. This species is also known to "double-clutch", laying multiple egg sacs from a single mating.

Mature Male

Mature Female

SCIENTIFIC NAME	# Psalmopoeus pulcher
COMMON NAMES	Panama Blonde

ORIGIN **Panama**

TYPE
New World, Arboreal, Webber

TEMPERAMENT
Unpredictable, fast and defensive

LIFESPAN
Females (10 to 12 years) | Males (3 to 4 years)

ADULT SIZE
12cm to 14cm

GROWTH RATE
Fast

SUGGESTED ENCLOSURE TEMPERATURES
Winter (20 to 24°C) | Summer (26 to 28°C)

SUGGESTED ENCLOSURE HUMIDITY
60% to 80%

BASIC ENCLOSURE REQUIREMENTS: Arboreal set-up with 5cm to 10cm of substrate, a water dish and added vertical structures to attach webbing.

The Panama Blonde is a wonderful looking tarantula from the Psalmopoeus genus. They have light-blonde to pink-orange setae/hairs over most of their bodies, along with a very light-blonde coloured carapace and a cream coloured abdomen. They also have interesting dark accents that run from the carapace towards the black patch at the rear of the abdomen. Truly a gorgeous spider after a fresh molt.

As with many arboreal species, they need vertical spaces and structures to build their webbed shelters. Use vertical pieces of drift wood or cork bark that are buried about 5cm below the substrate and reach to the upper areas of the enclosure. They will quickly create a burrow at the base of the shelter and web further and higher away from it. As time passes, they will construct quite a large webbed fortress in and around the main shelter.

Remember, venom in Psalmopoeus species is considered medically significant and a bite from one of these is to be avoided at all costs. Psalmopoeus pulcher has been known to have both docile and defensive specimens so make sure to become familiar with your own to ensure your own safety during maintenance. They can be unpredictable and are also known to leap if they think that's where they will find safety.

Psalmopoeus pulcher are relatively easy to breed and usually make great mothers, they fiercely protect their egg sacs and feed their young very well. Males are lanky and dull compared to females but still have rusty-orange tipped tarsi/feet. Males vibrate at high speeds to attract a female's attention and females can be quite violent so males should be protected during mating if possible.

If mating is successful, females will lay an egg sac containing anywhere around 120 to 180 eggs. You can remove the egg sac for manual incubation from about 4 weeks or leave it with mom full term. She may also lay a second egg sac from a single mating, called "double-clutching", seen regularly with Psalmopoeus irminia – Sun Tiger tarantulas.

Mature Female

Stromatopelma calceatum

Feather Leg Baboon Tarantula, Featherleg Baboon

ORIGIN   Various territories across West Africa

TYPE	TEMPERAMENT
Old World, Arboreal	Very defensive, can be aggressive

LIFESPAN	ADULT SIZE	GROWTH RATE
Females (12 to 15 years) | Males (3 to 4 years)	14cm to 16cm	Fast

SUGGESTED ENCLOSURE TEMPERATURES	SUGGESTED ENCLOSURE HUMIDITY
Winter (20 to 24°C) | Summer (24 to 28°C)	60% to 80%

BASIC ENCLOSURE REQUIREMENTS: Arboreal set-up with 5cm to 10cm of substrate, a vertical shelter like hollow cork bark or bamboo and a water dish.

"StroCal's" are large arboreal baboon spiders with long feathery legs and tarsi/feet. They have beautiful spotting and striping across their olive bodies with a starburst pattern on the carapace. Strictly not for beginners and recommended for experienced hobbyists only, the Feather Leg Baboon is an old world species with a reputation that well precedes it. This tarantula is known to be fast, very defensive and even aggressive if provoked. It will gladly deliver a painful envenomed bite. No solid medical data has been collected regarding the effects of this tarantula's venom on humans, but it's venom is considered medically significant, causing intense pain and burning which spreads, causing large areas of pain and cramping. Although they have a bad reputation they're not crazed violent tarantulas, anyone who considers keeping them should simply respect and understand what they are working with. With experience, you'll learn how to deal with their speed and temperament and will develop your own methods that ensure your safety. A simple example is to always place the enclosure of this species in a bath tub during maintenance so it has plenty space to move in case it should bolt and escape, giving you enough time and space to catch it safely and return it to it's enclosure.

There are no special requirements for breeding this species except for their regular comfortable environmental needs. Mating is an intense affair, males approach a female with pedipalp tapping, bobbing up and down and quick vibrations from their bodies. The female might attack or approach at high speed so be prepared for this. Once they engage, males will attempt to make inserts with both pedipalps if possible.

This is where you should be ready to protect him. If he doesn't get away fast enough after his insertions, it will be the end for him. If mating is successful, females will produce an egg sac fixed against their shelters a few months later. You can remove the egg sac at around 5 weeks if you choose to manually incubate the eggs and can expect anywhere from 200 to 280 eggs.

Mature Female

SCIENTIFIC NAME	Tapinauchenius cupreus
COMMON NAMES	Violet Tree Spider, Ecuador Tree Spider, Black & Gold Tree Spider

ORIGIN   Ecuador, Quito / Guyaquil

TYPE	TEMPERAMENT
New World, Arboreal	Nervous, defensive and fast

LIFESPAN	ADULT SIZE	GROWTH RATE
Females (12 to 16 years) | Males (3 to 4 years)	11cm to 12cm	Fast

SUGGESTED ENCLOSURE TEMPERATURES	SUGGESTED ENCLOSURE HUMIDITY
Winter (20 to 24°C) | Summer (24 to 28°C)	60% to 80%

BASIC ENCLOSURE REQUIREMENTS: Arboreal set-up with 5cm to 10cm of substrate, a vertical shelter like hollow cork bark or bamboo and a water dish.

Tapinauchenius cupreus is one of the faster moving species of Tarantula. From sling to adult, they can dart from one side of an enclosure to another in the blink of an eye. These are very sleek looking tarantulas with a metallic and almost silky appearance. Juveniles and freshly molted specimens can be dark purple or violet with a slight gold sheen over their bodies. As specimens progress through a molt cycle and also get to their older years, their dark purple becomes shrouded by a metallic golden overlay, making it evident why one of it's common names is the "Black & Gold Tree Spider". Their abdomens are also quite shiny and sleek in appearance with what look like little dimples nearer the spinnerets.

Tapinauchenius cupreus is a new world arboreal species which is more like an old world species in appearance and definition. They look more like an old world species, lack urticating bristles and their venom is medically significant. Bites are painful but said to be weaker than expected from an "Old-Word-Like" species. If you are new to old world arboreal species or looking to keep old world tarantulas, the Violet Tree Spider is a good introduction species for learning how to manage the speed, behaviour and temperament of species like Poecilotheria, Cyriopagopus, Stromatopelma, Heteroscodra and so on.

Breeding is relatively easy with this species and there are no special requirements to encourage a female to lay an egg sac. Males are dull and fluffy compared to females and will approach with a combination of tapping and vibrating. Females can be a little feisty but mating usually goes ahead quite smoothly. Protect your male just in case the female attacks. If mating is successful, the female will lay an egg sac containing anywhere from 100 to 200 eggs. The egg sac can be removed for manual incubation from around week 4 if you choose to do so.

Mature Female

SCIENTIFIC NAME	# Theraphosa stirmi
COMMON NAMES	Burgundy Goliath Bird-Eater

ORIGIN Guyana

TYPE
New World, Terrestrial, Opportunistic Burrower

TEMPERAMENT
Nervous, flicks urticating bristles

LIFESPAN
Females (18 to 20 years) | Males (3 to 5 years)

ADULT SIZE
26cm to 28cm

GROWTH RATE
Medium to Fast

SUGGESTED ENCLOSURE TEMPERATURES
Winter (18 to 20°C) | Summer (20 to 24°C)

SUGGESTED ENCLOSURE HUMIDITY
70% to 80%

BASIC ENCLOSURE REQUIREMENTS: Large terrestrial set-up with 20cm to 30cm or more of substrate with a deep, long shelter and a large water dish. More advanced enclosure set-ups are recommended to ensure the comfort of this species.

The Burgundy Goliath Bird-Eater is another of the world's largest terrestrial tarantulas with leg-spans reaching up to 28cm. It's a rich dusty brown monster with reddish setae/hairs on the legs and abdomen with pink/red striping on the patella/knees. Theraphosa stirmi is similar to other Theraphosas except subtle differences. Theraphosa stirmi lack setae/hair on the patella and bottom of the legs. It's carapace is higher/thicker due to larger fangs. Slings only show "pink" feet/tarsi on leg pair 1 and 2 and their pedipalps are darker. This species is generally calm, but skittish when disturbed. If feeling threatened, they will flick urticating bristles and even display a threat pose. They're also known to "hiss" by stridulating/chafing the fine bristles between their fangs. The urticating bristles of Theraphosas are some of the worst to come in contact with, causing severe itching over the body and burning on the skin. Although they do spend time out in the open, they also spend a large amount of time in their shelters or burrows, only wandering around at night in search of food. Venom is expected to be mild like most new world species, except a bite from an adult female's huge fangs will be quite painful regardless of venom. Fortunately, bites are not common.

Breeding this species can be difficult. Even experienced breeders struggle to breed them successively.

Females can be temperamental, often known to attack and kill males and also for eating or destroying their egg sacs later on. Large deep burrows with cool temperatures and high humidity seem to be what they're after but it's no exact science yet. Egg sacs contain around 200 eggs and if you're lucky enough to get one, it might be a good idea to pull it away from the female immediately for manual incubation. Also, interesting to note is that mature males lack tibial spurs/hooks.

Mature Male

Mature Female

Xenesthis immanis

Colombian Lesser Black

ORIGIN Panama, Brazil, Colombia, Venezuela, Ecuador, Peru

TYPE
New World, Terrestrial, Opportunistic Burrower

TEMPERAMENT
Nervous, flicks urticating bristles

LIFESPAN
Females (12 to 15 years) | Males (3 to 4 years)

ADULT SIZE
18cm to 22cm

GROWTH RATE
Medium to Fast

SUGGESTED ENCLOSURE TEMPERATURES
Winter (20 to 22°C) | Summer (24 to 28°C)

SUGGESTED ENCLOSURE HUMIDITY
70% to 80%

BASIC ENCLOSURE REQUIREMENTS: Terrestrial set-up with 15cm to 20cm of substrate with a large shelter and a large water dish.

Xenesthis immanis are impressive tarantulas. They eat really well, comfortably taking two large roaches at a time as full-grown adults. As slings, they eat just as well and will grow quite fast, increasing significantly in size between molts and showing adult colouration as juveniles already. In our opinion, one of the most beautiful new world species out there.

Females have stunning black velvet legs, metallic purple colouring on the carapace a bad-hair-day fuzzy blonde abdomen. Mature males are far more colourful than females with brighter purples covering the entire carapace and femurs of their lanky legs. This species enjoys a large shelter and a moist environment with fresh air. If it's too dry, you might your tarantula parked over the water dish, letting you know more moisture is needed.

Breeding Xenesthis immanis is difficult, we don't know of many breeders that can say they regularly get successful egg sacs from this species. Even if all goes well from mating to egg laying, fertility rates can be terrible. Egg sacs only contain about 80 eggs and often only 10 or 20 might be viable fertilized eggs. Also, females regularly eat egg sacs or destroy them and we can only assume this is because she can detect her egg sac is a failure. It's safer to pull an egg sac and incubate it manually in the hope of saving any fertile eggs. Every one is precious. Like Theraphosa, large deeply buried shelters seem to be preferred by this species. We were able to encourage our mated female to lay an egg sac by allowing the enclosure to dry out slightly, keeping only a large water dish for moisture. Temperatures were lowered to around 18°C and humidity to around 50% for 2 months or so, then we gradually increased temperatures to 26°C and humidity to around 80%, an egg sac was produced about 4 weeks later but sadly, no eggs were fertile.

Mature Male

Glossary

Aggressive
Tarantulas that actively attack a threat instead of simply being defensive against it.

Arboreal
Living in trees. In the case of tarantulas, any species living a vertically inclined lifestyle.

Communal
Tarantulas capable of living together in a single enclosure or "communal" set-up.

Defensive
A tarantula that will stand it's ground and defend itself by any means.

Docile
Calm and slow to react or show any defensive or aggressive behaviour.

Fossorial
Living below ground, in burrows, tunnels or other below-ground shelters.

Femur
The portion of a tarantula's leg between the carapace/head and knees/patella.

Instar
A tarantula's growth stage calculated by the number of molts it's had since hatching.

Leg-span / DLS
Generally refers to total diagonal leg-span of a tarantula, i.e. from rear left to front right.

New world
Refers mostly to tarantulas found in Northern, Central and South Americas.

Old world
Refers mostly to tarantulas found in Africa, Europe and the East.

Palpal bulb
Spiky bulbs found on the front of a mature male tarantula's pedipalps used for storing sperm and used during mating to fertilize a mature female.

Pedipalps
The set of "arms" between a tarantula's front pair of legs and it's fangs. Used for tasks like holding prey while eating or to carry substrate when excavating a burrow.

Sac / Egg Sac
A cocoon spun from silk thread by a female tarantula which stores her recently laid eggs.

Skittish
Twitchy, jumpy or other sharply nervous behaviour.

Slings
Term used by tarantula hobbyists to describe spiderlings.

Spermatheca
Sexual organs of a female tarantula used to store sperm and fertilize eggs.

Terrestrial
Tarantulas that live on the surface and generally create shelters above ground.

Tibial hooks/spurs (apophysis)
A set of "hooks" beneath the front two pairs of legs on many, but not all mature male tarantulas. Used during mating to engage and lift a female, giving the male access to her genital areas.

Urticating Bristles
Allergen coated barbs/bristles/hairs found on certain species of tarantulas, used for defense.

Reader's Notes

Avicularia sp. Pucallpa - Pucallpa Pink Toe - Mature Female

Reader's Notes

Poecilotheria metallica - Sapphire Ornamental - Mature Female

Made in United States
Troutdale, OR
12/17/2024